C000061395

# DON'T
# FORGET
# 2004

# DON'T FORGET 2004

## Advertising secrets of an impossible election victory

JAYSHREE M SUNDAR

Vitasta
LET KNOWLEDGE SPREAD

Published by
Renu Kaul Verma
Vitasta Publishing Pvt Ltd
2/15, Ansari Road, Daryaganj
New Delhi-110 002
info@vitastapublishing.com

ISBN 978-93-90961-28-3
© Jayshree M Sundar
First Edition 2022

MRP ₹495

Edited by Manjula Lal
Design concept by Pooja Trehan Theeng
Cover and layout by Somesh Kumar Mishra
Printed by Vikas Computer and Printers, New Delhi

For Baba

You nudged me to go for advertising as a
profession.
It's been an enthralling journey—from practising it
to teaching it.

Always in my heart.

# CONTENTS

# FOREWORD

Atal Bihari Vajpayee is said to have remarked that the 2004 Lok Sabha election verdict was one which the winner had not expected, nor the loser anticipated. It was undoubtedly a huge surprise, for the Congress was not expected to emerge as the single largest party, let alone be the anchor of a ruling coalition that would be in power for the next ten years.

The Congress had every disadvantage imaginable. It had been out of power for almost a decade. Its finances were stretched thin. It did not have a prime ministerial face. It was up against a Prime Minister who was generally well-liked and well-regarded. It faced a party that had been in campaign mode for almost a year prior to the polls. The media had decided that Mr Vajpayee would return to office.

Yet the Congress won. Many explanations have been offered for the verdict. Hubris and over-confidence on the part of the BJP certainly played a role. Political decisions that Mr Vajpayee apparently wanted to take but finally did not may have cost him. But to my mind the Congress' political strategy of seeing the national election as an aggregation of state-level elections and having the right alliances with regional parties proved to be the decisive factor. The campaign style of its leaders, especially of its president, that stressed public outreach and not just rallies added to the effectiveness of the political strategy.

Jayshree Sundar tells the story of the Congress' marketing campaign for the 2004 elections as seen from her perspective. This was a campaign that underpinned the political strategy. She was from the advertising world which, for some five months, became part and parcel of the Congress' publicity 'war room'. Salman Khurshid and I interacted with her and her team on a daily basis. The consumer research and insights that were presented by them formed the basis of a powerful creative strategy. Her narrative is a valuable contribution to understanding how one of the most stunning upsets in recent Indian political history was engineered.

**Jairam Ramesh, MP**
Former Union Minister

**July 2014**

I have just finished a marathon class at the Indian Institute of Management (IIM), Shillong.

Stepping outdoors, I take in the cool breeze and walk to the little canteen to order a hot cup of tea. I check my phone. There's a missed call from my husband.

I call back. He's just getting off a flight. 'How was your morning session?' he asks.

'Tiring, I just took the Congress' case study. It was a marathon class—four hours.'

'Oh, that's strange,' he said. 'You know why? I had a top BJP minister on the seat next to me on the flight. We got talking and I told him you had worked on the 2004 elections. And guess what he said?'

My tea has arrived. I take a sip. 'What?'

The minister said, 'We have collected each and every piece of that campaign and have studied it threadbare.'

*Ah ha.*

I switch off the phone and sit under a tree. I reflect on what just happened in the class. All eyes focused, body language totally engaged, the standing ovation at the end of the session.

Every time I have taken this session in my classes all over India, I get the same reaction. My students alone know this story first-hand from me.

So far.

I feel this experience should reach a much larger audience. After all it had political and historical importance in India's journey, changing a billion people's lives.

I have laid it out for readers as it unfolded. It's the story of how an advertising agency works, the inside machinery, the assets—which are the people essentially, their minds, responsiveness and temerity. And, of course, the client.

And this narrative is unbelievable. Almost.

At the outset, I must say this is an account of a small team of people that helped create history. This is not about any personal political alignment.

It's my diary of events that transpired between January and May 2004.

It's the story of an agency that was tasked to halt a bullet train...

It's the story of an agency that was desperate to turn around its fate as well...

You will see as you turn the pages...

# CHAPTER 1

## THAT WINTER CALL

### 'MA'AM, THERE'S A CALL FROM CONGRESS'

Which friend is fooling me?

IT'S A BITINGLY cold morning in Delhi. As usual, I am not taking this weather well. The nice guys from the admin department are getting a small heater fixed in my office room. I am pre-occupied. A meeting is about to begin with my Vice President Ali Imran and Executive Creative Director Rupam Borah. This is the office of Leo Burnett Delhi which is in a verdant lane ending in a *cul de sac*. I also happen to be heading it.

We gather around the sitting area of my office room and get some hot coffee to hopefully stimulate a good discussion. The year has begun. We need plans. We need new business. We need revenues. It's almost a year since I joined the agency. My brief is to turnaround the Delhi operations after the largest client has shifted base to Mumbai. Obviously, this has left a gaping hole in the balance sheet.

We have managed to win a few small accounts and our finance books show us as financially independent. Just about. However, I want to play in the Big League. And to motivate myself, I often have silent conversations in my mind. *We have created a centre of excellence. It's just waiting for the right client to find us. But where? How?*

Things are now in place, I convince myself.

*A good team, though very young. A good attitude. A huge*

*willingness to do whatever it would take to succeed, and a hunger to do excellent work. Both creatively and strategically. I have this one year to prove myself and put my office on the map.*

Yet, deep down, I am anxious.

The meeting is halfway through and we as a management team realise that we need a big breakthrough. The Delhi market is exploding and all eyes are on us. Not just within India but at the Asia Pacific level as well.

Needless to say, we are feeling tense as we realise the task ahead. Discussions done with a focus to make clear action plans before we meet a couple of days later—we conclude the meeting.

I take the last sip of my second cup of coffee. Stare out into the weak sun beating down on the plants of the wraparound balcony outside my room. Feeling the weight bearing down on my shoulders as I think of the entire team outside who look up to me to bring in new clients, grow the office exponentially and pay them handsome salaries. More than anything, I want them to be proud of the place they work in.

The shrill ringing of the phone shakes me out of my thoughts. The buzzer beeps. Jasbir, my secretary, announces it's a call from the Indian National Congress. And a thought crosses my mind immediately: 'Which friend is fooling me?'

I take the call. It's a polite male voice. He introduces himself as Shamim and says he's calling from Salman Khurshid's office. *The ex-minister? THAT Salman Khurshid?* Shamim says, 'We have shortlisted your agency for a pitch. You have to prepare and come to us within a week with your presentation.' *Wait*

*wait wait. One week? Where's the brief?* He says there is no brief. 'You can study it and construct the problem and give us a solution.' *Huh?*

Now, this does not surprise me. Because there are a ton of clients who don't give a formal brief. Particularly in Delhi. But I still think I am being pranked. So, I use my presence of mind and quickly tell him that we are a multinational agency and don't accept pitch invitations without a formal letter. (Of course, we do.) He asks for the fax number saying, 'I will send you an invitation letter within an hour.' I put the phone down and wonder. I keep absolutely quiet and tell no one about this call. Still in disbelief.

Within 30 minutes I see Jasbir walking in with a piece of paper in her hand. She places it on my desk and leaves. It has arrived. A very formal missive on the Indian National Congress' letterhead inviting our agency for a pitch on 14 January for the communications strategy and advertising campaign for the 2004 general elections.

Now I realise this is no friend pulling a fast one.

I leave the room looking for Ali and Rupam. The client service department is empty; maybe everyone is out for meetings.

I cross over to the creative area where the Monday morning job meetings are in progress. I open Rupam's door and find some of our creatives in a huddle discussing the routine job list. I say, 'Guys, I just got a call from the INC. The Indian National Congress.' They looked at me silently. 'This could be our big one for this year.' *Looks like I am trying to convince myself.*

Still processing, I walk to my room, taking in the pretty colourful office. Somewhere music is playing. Someone is yelling across to someone else. The front door is swinging open-shut in a rush. People are dressed edgily. It's the everyday madness of an advertising agency.

Rupam finishes his job meeting hurriedly and comes across. He wants me to repeat what I just burst in and said in his room. I phone Ali, who is out for a meeting and tell him while Rupam listens. 'We are being invited to pitch for the Congress campaign'. After the discussions, earlier this morning, they are both stunned.

I decide to share this development with my boss in Mumbai, CEO Arvind Sharma. His first question to me is, 'Will they pay by cheque?' I say I assume so. He tells me we can't proceed on assumptions. 'You have to find this out first and foremost. We will not deal in cash.' I get it. *But how do I ask?*

'Jayshree, we are supposed to be pitching. We will be doing it for free like every other agency. There is no shame in asking. Just go ahead, pick up the phone and ask Salman Khurshid straight.'

*Hmm, easier said than done.*

I tell Jasbir to connect me to Shamim. I figure he must be a Congress loyalist who works with Salman Khurshid. I ask with trepidation to talk to Salman Khurshid and before I know it, he is on the line. I ask if I can meet him. Just for a few minutes. And to my surprise, he readily agrees. Gives me a time of 6 pm at the India International Centre annexe. The reason I don't ask on the phone about payments is the lack of even a one-line brief. All we have is an invitation letter.

5

I'm hoping under the pretext of this discussion we will spend at least a few minutes together so that we can ask a few pertinent questions. I ask Ali to join me for this meeting.

Reaching the IIC annexe is a challenge, dodging peak hour traffic in Delhi. But we arrive with two minutes to spare. In the car, we have already made a plan. In case he offers us tea, we must accept. For an obvious reason. Buying time.

To our surprise, we find Salman Khurshid already seated at a table. He's on time and ahead of us. Wow! He gestures to us to take our seats and comes straight to the point. 'Yes,' he says, 'what was it that you would like to discuss?' He offers us tea. *Brava*. 'Sure', Ali and I say in unison. Orders are placed and we settle down quickly. I look him straight in the eye and ask the uncomfortable question. 'I'm sorry, I don't know any other way to do this, so I have to ask upfront. How will the payments be made? We operate on nothing else but cheque payments.' Without missing a beat, he responds unfazed. 'I don't think it will be a problem. We just got our website done and have paid the creator fully by cheque.'

The tea pot comes along with a pretty tea cozy and we pour ourselves some much-needed warmth. I ask: 'Can we ask you a few questions as there doesn't seem to be a brief?' He says, 'Go right ahead.'

We ask about their strategy, their plans, what to focus on. And while he answers everything at a general level, he repeats, 'You people should tell us the problem or opportunity from your point of view and give us the solution.' We murmur something about a week being too tight. He responds: 'For the meeting on the 14th, start with your strategy. You can show the creative approach and advertisements later if you are stuck for time.'

All in all, it was a very nice polite meeting. On the way back, we agree that he seems like a nice man, and spoke like one of us. I guess we had a different impression of politicians.

But we are still starting from scratch. No stimulus from their side. So many issues. Where to even begin? The deadline of a week is looming ahead.

I decide to form a team from within the resources at the office to work on this pitch. Account management, creative, account planning, and ask Starcom, our media partner, to join the effort. Most of the team is in their twenties. Enthusiastic, but lacking experience. They would need guidance every step of the way.

We gather in the conference room. At the outset, I tell them, 'I know this political party arena is alien, as compared to our regular world of FMCG, Durables, Services and so on, you must be feeling mixed up. Are you? How many of you are familiar with this world? Follow it? Interested in it?'

As you might have guessed, the 15-20-member team follows the normal distribution curve of the population. The bulk say they are somewhat interested but are no experts, a few say they have very little interest and know nothing and just a few say it's their area of interest. Ali is standing in a corner. Quietly observing. At the end of this discussion, he puts up his hand saying, 'I know the situation. I will figure it out.' Rupam says enthusiastically, 'I know somewhat about politics, but the creative department and I will handle whatever is asked of us—let's win this.'

While I did not admit it to my team, I definitely fell into the moderate knowledge category of people.

Next thing I tell them is: Let's treat this as a brand. Indian National Congress or AICC is the company that has a brand—The Congress party. And let's use the basic tenets of strategy and planning that we use for all other brands.

At the start, we all know that brands need to be known, or in marketing terms have Salience. If they are not on top of your mind, you don't remember them or think about them. Not only that, they need to be relevant. A brand can keep shouting messages, however, if it does not connect with the consumer it will never be of personal significance. Most of all, brands need to be 'Differentiated'. If you are a copy of someone else's agenda and brand world then you are an imitation. So, the Brand Equity blocks of Salience, Relevance and Differentiation will have to be applied to build Brand Resonance or the point where the consumer embraces the brand and actually becomes an ambassador for it, recommends it, believes in it.

The account planner's body language, I notice, shows reticence. I'm immediately on alert that there is a unique challenge with taking on a brand that is a political party. It's the world of ideology and it's hard to reconcile your personal beliefs with your professionalism.

I counsel my team, telling them upfront, 'Let's address the elephant in the room. I know some of you may be aligned to the opposite party and may find it hard to work on this.

However, in this profession I have had to work on blades and razors, hard liquor, male innerwear and many others. Likewise, men work on sanitary napkins, lipstick and female apparel. We have all worked on things we don't understand fully or can't identify with. So even with this, we have to be professional and treat it like a brand we have been assigned to work on.'

Seems like it's making sense. The team is excited. It's now inching closer to 10 pm. I end the meeting and tell everyone to go home, rest and come back fully charged. The next few days are going to be madly action-packed.

On the way home, my mind is racing. A million thoughts are buzzing. Primary amongst them is the need to quickly track my learnings on this subject. *How am I to lead a team or to talk with expertise with the client if I am not on top of my game?*

## DAY 2, 7 AM

A new day dawns. Freezing but determined to catch the newspaper delivery boy. I am pacing on the balcony. I spot him and instruct him to deliver 14 newspapers from the next day. All languages and regions covered. Of course, national papers too. And national weeklies. Pro- and anti-establishment. I have a quick bowl of oats with the news blaring away. My self-education has begun. I am going to absorb every word and sound bite possible. In all my spare time, I only discuss this topic. I keep picking people's brains and dissecting their viewpoints.

I reach the office and gather the team for a meeting. I spot a face with bloodshot eyes: Young Amit. I ask, 'Have you not slept?' He says, 'Actually I have not. I mapped the entire country. State by State. I looked at political coalitions and possible coalitions in the future. I studied each state and their burning issues.' *Wow.*

That's what you call a bright young spark. Two years out of MICA. Very intelligent. And clearly, a self-starter. Of course, with Ali's guidance, I am sure.

The next two days see some frenetic working and brainstorming. A process of discovery is slowly but surely unfolding.

What do we find? The 'India Shining' campaign for the Government of India has already run for three months. It is estimated that a sum of Rs 300 crore has already been spent on it, though the official figures being quoted are way lower. Suffice to say it's huge. Large-sized newspaper advertisements in colour and long television commercials are bombarding the Indian consumer. Non-stop. Relentless. Everyday. Interspersed in the visuals of happy families are lofty statements of how high the stock market has reached, and how unprecedented the forex reserves are, how the economy has grown by 10.6 per cent and how there is a stirring of peace with our neighbour ushering in never before stability. How development is galloping. And many more such endorphin-releasing statements.

The chattering classes in urban India are excited. From drawing rooms in Lutyens Delhi and posh homes in Mumbai's Malabar Hills to the bungalows in Chennai's Boat Club Road and such-like, there is positive chatter—the kind that only comes when the urban elite is in approval.

# Happy
## New Year.

You are now stronger and prouder with
## $100 billion shining.

Schools are breathing.
Children are sparkling.
Future is inspiring.

You've never had
a better time to shine long.

india
Sh|ning

I make my
India shine.

india
Sh|ning

india
Sh|ning

We get down to very detailed secondary research. All of us are digging and investigating into all forms of published data available. Finding intelligent pathways through heaps of published material is an art in itself. Since we are asking the right questions, the correct data is being thrown back at us. No one is too senior or junior for this task. So around five or six of us are carving out information which will form the basis of strategic discussions. We decide to convene again.

At this meeting, we summarise the Top Lines of the research we have done so far.

Our findings are enumerated as follows:

1. The government's confidence is based on a series of opinion polls carried out by different research agencies and media, most of which have also forecast that the number of Congress seats in Parliament would decline, with some saying that the number could go from the current 112 to as low as 75 (out of a total of 542).

2. The media and poll experts surmise that the Congress' best bet is to hope that its seat tally will not fall. A party which has led India's freedom struggle and ruled the country for almost 50 years after independence is being criticised and written off by opinion-makers.

3. Congress has just been swept out of power in three key northern states in the Assembly elections held in December 2003. Importantly, the 2004 elections, earlier scheduled for September-October, have been advanced to April-May. The ruling government is extremely confident of winning by a landslide, riding

on the popularity of its leader Atal Bihari Vajpayee, and strong economic growth.

Over sips of coffee, the penny drops, and the conversation in the room is animated.

*'Guys, do you realise this is the biggest brand re-launch ever?'*

*'This must be the largest target audience in the world any advertising has to be done for! Every 18+ Indian!'*

As the meeting progresses, some very pertinent data points are emerging.

What do we find?

First, we find that the employment exchange is groaning under the weight of job applications: 43 million people registered. Promises of creating 1 crore plus jobs have not happened. Unemployment is at an all-time high. This is a major data point.

Second, we find farmer suicides have increased exponentially due to very high loan rates, poor irrigation and prices of crops.

Third, we find that the middle-class investor has lost precious life-time savings in the US64 scam and Kisan Vikas Patra scam.

Fourth, we find no significant schemes for the upliftment of women despite women forming 48 per cent of the population.

Fifth, we find food is rotting in Food Corporation of India godowns while many go hungry. Data throws up the fact that 300 million people don't earn enough to eat one square meal a day.

And so, on and so forth. We quickly form a hypothesis. And the hypothesis is this.

*All this points to a class of people for whom India is not shining.*

*And, therefore, are not listening. Can we get them to listen to us?*

*Is there a Brand Bond we can form between the party and its consumers?*

*And who will these consumers be?*

We need to talk to the people who constitute the unserved market. Everyone who struggles for day-to-day survival. The semi-urban and rural consumer. Both men and women. Young and old. This is a potential target audience for our campaign as we are beginning to figure.

And it is exactly at this point that I think our core strategy emerges.

Sitting in the comfort of a conference room in Delhi and having debates is all very well. However, nothing is proven until it emerges from the horse's mouth.

We need to contact consumers who we believe are left out of the 'feel-good' narrative.

Urgently. Quickly.

Time is racing by.

The question is, how?

We have to get under the skin of the consumer. Figure out their thinking. Data-mine consumer insights.

We need to test our hypothesis. Nothing will proceed without consumer contact. That we are clear on. Secondary research will carry on for sure, but we need to confirm directly from the consumer. Have some people really not been touched by the high-decibel propaganda?

We hit upon a breakthrough idea. Why don't we send people out across the country and get some primary research done? The agency team members are busy with so much going on with this pitch and their regular clients. We would not be able to spare so many executives. Going to an external agency would be a big-time commitment. We are also worried about confidentiality and leaking of information.

Currently, I am also teaching a one-year programme at TSM (Times School of Marketing). Teaching has been my passion. I do it on weekends and have a good vibe with my students. Their winter internship happens to be for three weeks in January. Vispy Saher, the dynamic principal of TSM, tells me many of the students want to intern at my agency. He requests me to comply if possible. I agree readily with a caveat. We will not be able to pay a stipend. Of course, all expenses on actuals will be settled. Not that I want to be cheap—we just don't have the extra funds. About 14 TSM trainees invade the office. Apart from adding some colour, there is a lot of energy in the air with so many enthusiastic people around. Being my students, I know their calibre. I have handpicked the best to join the agency.

The troupe of TSM trainees march in looking rather tense, as if they are about to be admonished for some misdemeanour. We tell them to relax.

We sit them down and tell them that they are going to be a part of something very important. Their eyes light up in anticipation. They are going to test a theory we are formulating which will form the crux of the strategy we will be proposing to the client on the 14th.

Seven teams of two students with a cameraman are sent out early the next morning to different parts of the country. They are briefed very clearly and thoroughly. We tell them to keep it strictly confidential. The job at hand is simple but critical. Nobody should know who they are representing. We educate them on the target audience for the survey. Respondents, both men and women, are to be selected from the middle to lower-middle to poor sections of society. Go only to semi-urban and rural areas. Why? Because Urban India has bought into 'India Shining', or so we think at this point. We have no idea what the rest of India is thinking. We need to find out quickly.

We have five days left before the presentation. Early next morning, the teams leave for their destinations. A few of our executives also are on some of the teams. They are armed with just three pertinent questions for the in-camera interviews and a separate quantitative questionnaire. We expect them back within two or three days.

Meanwhile, in Delhi, the rest of us carry on with our pitch preparation. I find that the account planner has made zero contribution. More than the others, he has had a difficult time separating his own beliefs and being professional about his choices. He can't bring himself to work on this. I have no choice but to drop him from this pitch and free him up to work on something he can dedicate himself to in a happier way.

Early mornings, I now scan 14 newspapers. Even though I cannot understand many regional languages, I see the pictures and figure out the top stories being covered in each state. I gobble up the television news in Hindi, Bengali, Marathi,

Tamil and even Gujarati, as I have a decent understanding of these languages. While I feel more confident, it is not enough. I seek confidential meetings with experts, whom I will refrain from naming here. Suffice it to say they were people of high repute, balanced professionals with no vested interests. Ali, of course, is part of these meetings. We both go with our diaries and questions and take notes furiously.

Without telling them our line of inquiry, we ask questions to check our hypotheses.

Ali and I mull over the discussion in the car after one such meeting. His insights into the issues in each state and the history of the reforms of 1991 are sharp, crystal clear. This was the historic year when the dream budget was delivered by Dr Manmohan Singh in Parliament, opening up India's economy to foreign investment and companies. In the office, he is my bouncing board on political issues. Things seem to be coming into focus. A picture is emerging about where we should take the fight.

He makes a good point as we inch ahead on the long drive back. 'Jayshree, everything can be done. But remember there is one major hurdle for the Congress. We will be fighting a Prime Minister at the peak of his popularity. Atal Bihari Vajpayee is respected and loved, is seen as unable to do wrong. Also, nuclear tests in Pokhran and the victory at Kargil have added to his image.'

'Yes', I sigh. 'You're right.' So far, no leader has been announced from the Congress. So far, the party is pitching itself as a team. But no leadership face.

Now we are back in office. Whenever a pitch is about to happen, the advertising market starts buzzing. The grapevine has it that eight agencies are in the fray. It is a mix of large, medium and small agencies. The media is very curious as this is a high-profile pitch, one that is happening suddenly as early polls have been called. As per schedule, the ballot should have been in September 2004. However, on the back of its massive Assembly victories, the BJP has called for elections before the due date.

The BJP is hoping to constitute the new House by March or latest early April. The Election Commission is yet to announce the dates when the voting will be held. Therefore, an agency being selected this late in the game is unprecedented.

Small agencies in a pitch are always a dicey adversary. Their cost structure being low and their owner being a one-man decision-maker make for a lethal combination. A lot can be promised without hierarchies and decisions can be taken on the spot. They usually hire freelance talent so they can manage a low fee to the client.

Large agencies come with power. In-house infrastructure. Legacy. Big names. It's for a client to decide if they want that badge value. Large agencies have hierarchies. And at times are slow as a result.

We are at best medium-sized. We are making a fresh start and our team has been in play for a year. We are in the process of reputation building and have got some low key but good media coverage—which is why we have been invited to pitch, is my guess. Our inside story of struggle is our own. The outer story is beginning to look good. We are a full-service agency and are going ahead for this pitch with Starcom, our media partner.

Starcom works out of the same premises in a separate office. They are led by Anita Nayyar, a veteran media expert, very well known in the industry. She is a go-getter and has good relationships with the press and television media. Fortunately, we knew each other from our previous stint at Lintas.

## DAY 3, 4 PM

Rupam, Ali and I are in a meeting, planning the boundaries of our pitch. We figure out that the same sort of brief has gone to all agencies. We also know that political parties rarely use agencies unless it's a general election. They are not regular clients of advertising agencies. So, it would be best to make things very clear in terms of strategy, research, creative and media, not leaving anything to the imagination.

So, while they are saying tell us your strategy, we decide not to take it at face value. One key decision that gets taken at that meeting is that we will go for the entire campaign. The full package. Strategy and creative. And media approach. So that it's easy for them to comprehend what we mean. End of the day, the offering of an advertising agency is its creative product based on sound, solid strategy. One without the other doesn't make sense. Especially to people who don't deal in this field— and, more importantly, are running out of time.

This is a tall order. We are five days away from the

presentation. We are waiting for the research findings. We are all formulating ideas. But we need ratification.

Meanwhile, Shamim calls us a couple of times a day to check in. I have done my reference check on him. I find out that he is a scholar from JNU and joined the Congress party as he was very inspired by Rajiv Gandhi. They are located at South Avenue diagonally opposite Teen Murti Bhawan. On one such call I ask if Amit, our young executive, can come and meet him. He readily agrees.

My brief to Amit is to check out the address where we would be presenting. What is the room like? How much space? Amit looks baffled. He is ready to go but wonders why I need to know all this. I explain to him, 'Pitching is all about control and comfort with your environment. If, for example, we don't have proper facilities we are going to waste precious meeting time allotted to us trying to set up. They have given a time slot of 30 minutes for the presentation. We must know what we are in for.'

We now get the news that some of the research teams are on their way back.

Meanwhile, back to brainstorming, ideating and discussing.

Honing our strategy further, we make the following discoveries.

1.  We have figured out that the reform issue is cloudy. Liberalisation and the dream budget which opened up the economy in 1991 is not fully credited to the Congress in the younger consumesr' mind. They are not aware that it was under the Congress-led government that the

economy was liberalised. In 2004, with the party out of power for nine years, public memory is fading that they were the architects of economic change.

Interestingly, the incumbent BJP-led government is getting credit for these radical reforms, even though they were a result of economic reforms introduced by the Congress during its most recent stint in power (1991-96). However, the Congress stands little chance of being able to recapture the credit due to it. With 54 per cent of the population below the age of 25, there is virtually no recall of the Congress' achievements or ideology. The ruling government is using this to its advantage, stating that it had achieved more during its five years in power than the Congress in fifty years.

2. We focus on the fact that while they are not the ruling party at the Centre, Congress is still ruling in eleven states.

3. We know that gamechangers like the Green Revolution which aided the farmers or the White Revolution which boosted milk supply, or the creation of Public Sector Undertakings, and higher education offerings like the Indian Institute of Technology, Indian Institute of Management, nuclear and space developments through ISRO and so many economic developments were undertaken in the erstwhile Congress regimes. But these facts are now buried deep down somewhere. Putting it another way: Not on anyone's radar screen. As I said earlier, the reforms and development issues are

cloudy.

4. Very pertinent to note is that the new voter in the age bracket of 18-22 qualifying to vote for the first time would have been quite young when developmental reforms and liberalisation came in. Therefore, they are likely to think all the positives accrue to the current ruling party. And that's natural.

5. We also are investigating the situation on the ground. The Congress party is not in good shape at all performance-wise. They got a drubbing in the Assembly elections held in December. Three states went to polls: Rajasthan, Haryana and Chhattisgarh. All resulted in massive losses.

6. And of importance is that India has a population of over a billion, but only approximately 30 per cent of this is urban. The balance 70 per cent lives in rural areas and is primarily dependent on agriculture for its livelihood. Even in urban areas, while there has been an upswing in incomes and living standards, big chunks of the population live a difficult life, burdened with large families and their economic expectations.

7. While the stock market had touched new heights, small investors had lost their life savings in a government securities-related scam.

8. Similarly, the government has committed to creating 10 million jobs every year, but the number of unemployed people has gone up every year.

9. Also, the government has announced many farmer

welfare schemes, but hundreds of farmers across the country have committed suicide due to their inability to pay off their debts.

10. Virtually nothing of value has been done for the welfare of women. This whole area has been woefully neglected.

What about alliances and coalitions?

We revisit the political map of India, state by state to study each one's issues separately.

We realise that lack of coalition alliances has kept the Congress party out of power for over nine years.

On the contrary, the BJP has already forged alliances with regional forces to form the National Democratic Alliance (NDA) and is going into the election as a joint force.

We figure out that the Congress party has understood that alliances will be required, and this was alluded to in the Shimla and Srinagar meetings in 2003, where a clear message was sent out to forge partnerships with secular and like-minded parties, especially regional ones. A lot of work still has to be done on that front. Things are not very clear at this point to us and digging into newspaper reports does not shed any more light on this.

11. The ruling party, the BJP, has been talking of a 'feel good factor' and has run an aggressive campaign on this theme. An avalanche of rupees is being spent. The Indian consumer cannot miss the onslaught

of communication. There is total silence from the Congress.

12. Momentum is gathering on murmurings about the 'foreigner issue' and decibels are rising. Sonia Gandhi has taken over the reins of the Congress party firmly and from what we gather is respected within the rank and file of the organisation. Her public persona and interaction have been very low key with the people of India. So far. People opposed to her are building a dialogue on her not being qualified to be in public office due to this reason.

## DAY 3, 8 PM

As our meeting carries on non-stop, a bit of fatigue sets in. It's pitch dark outside. Some music is playing in the office. Somewhere. Just then, there is a welcome diversion.

Amit has returned after many hours. 'Where have you been? Why so long?' He is like that guest who has arrived from a foreign country. We all surround him and want to know what transpired. He says he saw Salman Khurshid, Jairam Ramesh, Ambika Soni, Ahmed Patel, Motilal Vora (Congress leaders) and a couple of others in discussion in the front room of the South Avenue premises. He described the place as a four-room ground floor bungalow. A tiny kitchen, one common bathroom, and three smaller rooms. Not too much activity. This is what they refer to as their war room. Goodness!

A thought crosses all our minds. While advertising has

been relentless from the BJP, their Public Relations machinery has also been churning out interesting stories. The Indian consumer learns about the concept of the War Room. The BJP has the seasoned Pramod Mahajan in charge. He is considered dynamic and tough. We see pictures of a very smart office, an obviously busy place, lined with computers, people rushing around. Almost a quasi-set-up of people preparing for battle.

But back to Amit and the news he has brought on the presentations.

Now when he asks Shamim in which room the presentations are lined up, to his surprise the answer is 'Not here.' Oh.

'So where? AICC?'

'No. A bungalow in Lodhi Estate.'

It's the residence of a Mumbai-based Minister of Parliament, who is not in the city and has allowed the presentations to take place there. He has an office room annexed to his bungalow.

Now Amit asks a direct question. 'Can we go and see it, please?' Shamim is caught off guard. He says no other agency is asking these questions. 'Why do you need to go?'

Amit replies about his boss (me) being very particular about these things and would not like him to return without seeing the place.

Shamim relents. 'Give me a bit of time. Let me wind up a couple of things and we can leave.' The hidden powers of a woman in charge! They didn't know how to deal with my demands. So might as well give in.

Once they reach the venue at Lodhi Estate they see a huge lawn and the main house. There is a fairly large office area on the side of the house—stand-alone and delinked from the main residence. They enter and Amit makes a quick assessment. He thanks Shamim and leaves.

Back in the office, I ask him if there is enough wall space to project the slides of our presentation. He says, 'The room is pretty fancy. Paintings and artefacts and sculptures all around.'

*It would be a waste of time to re-do someone's office to project our slides. I mean imagine all of us busy removing paintings from walls!*

I make a quick decision. We will hire our tried and tested equipment supplier to accompany us to this meeting. He will carry a big screen and a 29-inch television to project the presentation slides and ancillaries.

Shamim, who has become quite a good liaison man between the client and agency, calls to reconfirm the presentation. I, of course, put on my bullet-proof persona and say we are on. But inside, my stomach churns. *So much to do. So little time.*

It's the usual story before any pitch. But the queasiness factor has tripled for this one because of the audience. Politicians whom we have seen on television. The people we read about every day in the news. This isn't your normal or garden variety of marketing vice president or brand manager.

I ask him upfront as to how many agencies are pitching. He is direct in his reply. 'Eight, in total. Half an hour each.' I do a quick calculation. It means the client team would be hearing four hours of different plans and presentations. With even ten minutes for a gap between two agencies, that would total to six hours. I decide we would not want to be in the middle.

Too much of a mishmash. Going in first is always a good idea to create an impact but we needed every extra hour to get our work to be stellar. They were scheduling the meetings starting at 2 pm. I requested the last slot.

My learnings on the numerous pitches I had done in my erstwhile agency Lintas was to take the first or last slot. Always helps when there was a series of meetings discussing the same topic non-stop. Somehow it always works to get you noticed. Whether you make it to the next round or not depends purely on your content and vibe. Again, Shamim is nonplussed but agrees. He tells me no one else has asked. 'I am deciding the order. Since you are asking, I will give you the last slot.' *No harm in asking, right? Gets you where you want to be.*

I put down the phone and reflect. *I hope he keeps his word.* Relationships at the client's end, up and down the order, are very important. Often in my experience, I have seen how junior managers can create havoc and unhappiness with their current agency and get the bosses to call for a pitch. If they take to you, they manoeuvre things around in your favour. They are important.

It's approximately 9 pm. I make a quick call home and check in on the family.

I head to the conference room where the first of the teams from Rajasthan and UP have returned. They are tired but also very excited. Meeting with the actual consumers is always very revealing because you see them answer your questions on camera. And the recordings of those interviews from small towns and villages is what we are about to witness right here in Delhi.

The Vox Populi (voice of the people) interviews on camera had just three questions.

1. Have you heard of India Shining or Bharat Uday?
2. Has your life changed in the last five years?
3. If so, how?

There is also a longer quantitative questionnaire which the teams have filled up.

As the entire team huddles around the television, the videographer puts on the raw footage for all of us to see. We ask him to wait outside.

Remember the people we had defined as our target groups?

Semi-urban, rural, men and women.

Small traders, shopkeepers, self-employed, farmers and such like.

The footage starts rolling. And the findings are astounding. Person after person says the same thing.

*Most of them have no clue about India Shining or Bharat Uday. They don't recall seeing it.*

Yes, their life has changed in the last five years.

And they all say, '*Bahut bekar ho gaya hai.*' (It has become worse.)

As more and more of our research teams return to home base, we are finding absolute consistency in the responses.

The answers are overwhelmingly similar.

As an aside, the footage was stunning. The rustic beauty of India. Fields. Small homes. Real faces. Colourful clothes and turbans. Farmers of every region wear different *pagris* (turbans). I marvel at this while watching the hours and hours of footage. From Bangalore, Pune, Meerut, Alwar, Delhi and many more places.

I am very excited with these findings. They corroborate our surmises.

Dinner gets ordered from the nearby *dhaba*. *Rotis, dal tadka, aloo gobi* and chicken *kebab*. People grab a bite and keep watching the tapes. More and more of the same. So much latent distress. A feeling of being sidelined. Of being compromised. A few voices here or there would not be considered significant. But everyone without fail from obscure parts of the country is saying the same thing.

A pattern is forming. A thought process is taking shape.

The beginning of a pitch strategy unfolding right there as the consumer ratifies our hypothesis.

Now, it's well past midnight. We have pre-booked the editing studio. The owners have agreed to keep it open all night. Ali and I form a team of three executives. They are briefed in detail—the length of the Vox Populi, the number of respondents and how to edit answers.

Our attempt is to show as many faces as possible, from all the regions to which the team travelled. To put in the meat, we have found out. We are very clear that it should not look like only a few people were contacted for a self-serving purpose. We need intelligent, detailed editing.

The team is charged up. They assure us they would take care of it. As they are about to leave, we discuss confidentiality issues. They would bring back each and every tape of raw footage. They would delete all material from the hard disk at the studio. That sorted and a late dinner done, they set off for what will be an endless night.

## DAY 4, 1 AM

The night is still. It's misty outside. We settle down for our last discussion of what has been a long long day in Rupam's room. His room is interesting. Creative people always have interesting posters and knick-knacks. There is a bean bag in a corner on which Ali sits. I look around. There are loads of sketch books, CDs, resumes, production reels, a telephone shaped like 'Kermit The Frog', trophies, bunch of black Pentel sketch pens, Archive magazines, a frame with photos of daughters and dogs, a dinky diecast Corvette Shark...He opens the drawer in his desk and pulls out some chocolate. We bite into some sugar rush.

The three of us are planning what needs to happen in the morning and the rest of the day. *Three and a half days left until the meeting. That's very little time.*

Given we want to carry a full-blown package of strategy, creative and media. Not one pen has been put to paper yet. *But how can that happen till the thinking is clear? And how could the thinking be clear until the research was done?*

We decide to give ourselves a little credit for the ground we have covered so far. We decided to convene at 9.30 am and have a creative briefing session by 11.30 am.

Finally, it's time to head home. The streets are empty. A

dog barks somewhere in the distance. I check my SMS feed. I think of the boys at the editing studio. I realise I will get a maximum of four hours of sleep if I get lucky.

# CHAPTER 2

## 'WE NEED A WINNING IDEA'

# DAY 4

COUNTDOWN TO PITCH BEGINS!

As I drink my tea, dunking biscuits in it and leafing through the 14 papers, I prepare myself for the day. Plough through a boring bowl of oats with the television news blaring in front of me. The political battle is heating up. Regional power centres are being subjected to the national gaze. BSP, Left Front, DMK, AIADMK and so many more.

The office is buzzing early in the morning. As I enter the reception, I see the blushing red apples on the reception counter, a norm at every Leo Burnett office worldwide. It's a very important day for us. The client service and planning team and I get into a meeting. We need to craft the problem statement to formulate a sharp creative brief.

The creative team is waiting. They need to start work. They are restless and tense and wonder how they will complete the task in time. These are crunch deadlines.

Let me summarise what we have been discussing:

First, we define who will be the focus of the campaign. We decide to head to the blue ocean. In other words, the part of the market where there are no players. Where the waters are clear. Let me elaborate on what that means as this is very important.

Very simply put, we decide to go to the unserved market. The market as we now know is untouched by India Shining. That is what we decide is the unserved market. What does this mean?

We decided to take the fight regional. We decide 90 per cent of our campaign will run in Indian languages and to that consumer who is not primarily English speaking. Very little in English. This is a brave strategy albeit a differentiated one.

Setting target audience is very important in any advertising and communication task. Who are you talking to? What are they thinking right now? What key messages do you want to give them? And why will they have an interest in listening to you? It is always easy to say let's go to everyone. And if budgets are unlimited, that's a possibility. But in the real world, one has to prioritise.

Now here is the degree of difficulty. And a very unique one. In all other brand communications, you have a group of consumers who form a set. For example, carbonated drinks are consumed by teenagers and young adults, shampoos with dandruff removing agents have an audience who suffer from the problem. Hair colour is for the fashionable and those who are greying, business newspapers for corporate office-goers, four-wheel drive cars for the adventurous and image-conscious.

But here the issue is much larger. Why?

As I told you earlier, this is the largest target audience in the world. Perhaps 650 million people eligible to vote.

Every Indian is a potential target. Every 18+ Indian.

Given the population is at one billion and India is a young country, that will add up to millions of people.

And another penny drops. The usual 80:20 rule doesn't

apply here. What I mean by that is, in a lot of product categories, it is proven that 20 per cent of consumers give you 80 per cent of sales. The 20 per cent who are predisposed to the category and your brand. Those who have the buying power. They repeat purchases and are that precious set of consumers who you cherish and keep creating enticing messages for. They love you. They buy you. They are your believers. Marketing people are always researching these profiles of people and creating value for them. In turn, they give you the bulk of your revenues. The relationship is symbiotic.

*With this brand, a political party, it is different. The key point we note is that there is no repeat purchase. Everyone has one vote. And everyone is equal. Rich, poor, old, young, rural, urban, semi-urban, semi-rural, women and men.*

One vote. One voting day. Will they go out from their houses and make the effort? Will they not? If they don't, the power in their hands to make a difference perishes.

As we keep drilling, we figure out some very telling and surprising trends. What are these and how do they form the contours of our thinking? On delving and researching we find that the urban Indian consumer is pretty inert on Voting Day. Data shows that approximately 55 per cent of India goes to vote. The rest just stay away. Our sense is that much more of rural India casts its precious ballot.

Our research also points to that fact. Every respondent we ask says they will go to vote. The middle class and below that.

Now being clear on this aspect, we have to make some tough calls. In an ideal world with endless budgets, we would want to reach every person in media terms. We want the advertisements and messages to be seen multiple times by our targeted consumer. That is the concept of OTS (Opportunity To See). And that concept teaches us that the greater number of times a message is seen, the more likely it is to be retained in the brain. And that any pre-disposed action can only follow after that.

But our judgment tells us that for a party out of power for nine years, there may not be endless funds. We are sure of it. So as in consumer brands, you have to create priorities towards the most pre-disposed and point your message towards them. We, therefore, create a primary and secondary audience.

We decide we will talk to four target groups who we know are hurting the most.

Farmers
Unemployed youth
Middle-class petty investors
Women

These four classes of people have had little attention paid to them or active policies to support them.

- Farmers are in the doldrums. Many have died by suicide and left behind large families.
- Young people to whom jobs have been promised yet are still jobless are frustrated and disgruntled.
- Middle-class families have lost precious savings. The

economic outlook for them is bleak. The rising cost of living is not helping.

- Women. Making up almost half our staggering population. Nothing of note for them either.

To top it all 'India Shining' is elitist and boastful. It perhaps targets to international markets to showcase financial progress over the past five years. And has ignored the voice of the consumer. It's more what is termed a 'manufacturer's statement'. Our research clearly shows it is a claim. Because it has not touched the lives of the middle class and the poor.

Cracking the strategy to a complicated problem is always challenging. It is a part of the job we love. And it's all about gut feel. When you study an issue thoroughly and make intelligent pathways. When your mind deduces the right notes. When key people in your team rally around the thought process. When everyone starts getting invested and starts adding layers.

That's what is unfolding right here.

Having got some pillars of thinking in place, we move to the next step. We have to focus on the messages and the pitch.

Just then my boss Arvind calls. He is in his car on the Mumbai-Pune highway. He asks me where we have reached in our thought process. I have been discussing the strategic fact-finding progress and our hypotheses with him on a daily basis. Updating him on our insights and research. I summarise all the findings and the slant of our thoughts as a result. With everything he has heard so far, he gives an interesting take on who to write the brief for.

*'Bus mein latakta hua aadmi.'*

'The man who takes the bus to work.'

How would we describe him?

The man who takes a bus to work. Is always in a rush. Has no option but to cling on to the rails and somehow make the journey. The man who struggles day-to-day.

We use the advertising goalpost of Target Person. Once this is defined, we know it will get easier for the creative teams to do the campaign. For the copywriters to write the lines and the art directors to plan the visuals. Because the man who hangs from the bus and struggles everyday conjures up images and a tone of voice, that makes it easy for the creative teams. Thank you, Arvind, for your call at an opportune moment.

So, it is not literal. Not just people who are squashed in buses. But all people like them who struggle every day.

This, we are sure encompasses the middle class to the poor. Strivers and the destitute.

Common everyday people struggling to make ends meet. Those who have lost hope.

Now it's time to write a formal brief. The client service team creates a sharp, clear and focused one.

What does the creative briefing document state?

Let me enumerate the points.

- A regional campaign. Therefore, multiple languages across the country. Speak to the consumer in his idiom. For the purposes of the pitch, we decide to carry the bulk of the creatives in Hindi. Usually, languages are translated using a main language as the base. That would come at a later stage. Provided they approve of us as their advertising partner and we work with them.

- We also decide not to have only an anti-incumbency campaign. That would be limiting and negative. So, it's clear we needed phases for our campaign.

Some quick calculations. We are pretty certain that the campaign would start by the middle of February given that the first round of the pitch has still not happened. What happened, in reality, is another story! More about that later.

We plan for three phases of communications.

The Questions phase
The Reintroduction of Congress phase
The Vision phase

- And while 90 per cent of the budget as we see it would be regional, we do realise that the urban consumers need to be addressed. The ones sitting on the fence. Those who may need some nudging to rethink. So, we would have to think of a campaign for this group. Not the primary focus but not to be ignored either. This is what we call the Ambush campaign.
- We are going to recommend telling them to keep the advertising clean and honest. But in case too many salvos get fired from competitive sources, we should keep a minuscule budget for retaliatory ads. Our recommendation would be to not get it murky and

stick to our gameplan. We have our work cut out there.

• One of the most important aspects of a Political Advertising Campaign is the slogan. Absolutely and critically important. A good slogan gets currency with the public like wildfire. It needs to cut across all sections of the population. The current slogan of the Bharatiya Janata Party, India Shining, has made the cut with urban India. Our research shows it has not quite enthused the middle to lower class of the population.

Margaret Thatcher won the elections in 1980 on the power of the slogan 'Labour Isn't Working', considered one of the best political slogans of all time. Years later, Barack Obama struck gold with 'Yes We Can'. Closer home in India, some powerful slogans were Lal Bahadur Shastri's *Jai Jawan Jai Kisan* and Indira Gandhi's *Garibi Hatao*. Also *Ab ki Baari Atal Bihari*.

It's imperative we create a powerful slogan.

## 11 AM

The team that was editing the Vox Populi has returned to the agency. They look dead beat. Paranoid about secrecy, I double-check with them if they have brought back every trace of footage and material they had carried. They assure me they have. And before I can ask the next question, they assure me they have deleted everything on the hard drive at the editing suite and no one there has a clue what they worked on. I smile. Tired smiles come back.

We quickly put on the edit. Take a look at the film. It's about four minutes. Like a story. People answering questions. Absolutely well made. Honest. Truthful. Real. And explosive. Unhappiness and misery of the past five years from consumers' mouths.

## 11.30 AM

The creative teams walk into the conference room. Sleeves rolled up. Excited, anticipating a lot of work ahead. There are two senior art and copy teams. A competent Hindi copywriter Sanjiv and, of course Rupam, who heads the creative function.

The canteen boys are bringing in the tea.

The client service guys are ready. Ali is heading that team.

Now, this is a sacred meeting. No document in the advertising agency is as precious as a well-written brief. No internal meeting has as much tension as a briefing session for a major campaign. Why? Because the Planning and Servicing teams need to sell their thinking and excite the creatives into taking a leap to a level of adrenaline where the best can emerge. Usually, the creative guys are poker-faced at this meeting. They like to ask a lot of questions. Sometimes dent holes in the brief. They usually refuse to work on things they are not convinced about.

The briefing process begins. I sit at the head of the table quietly observing everyone. The tone of voice. Body language. Interest levels.

The creative team accepts the brief without any major issue. They ask a lot of intelligent questions to clarify matters in their heads. I figure that two of them are very well versed in the political scenario: Associate Creative Director and Koustuv Chatterjee, our Creative group head. Pooja Trehan Teeng is going to be the Senior Art Director on this campaign. She's had a lot of experience after graduating from a premium art college. In fact, the whole team adds a lot of value to the meeting.

The cherry on the cake is the fully edited Vox Populi with the real consumer. The television screen springs to life and the tape plays out. It's like the consumer has entered the board room. The creative guys who have not been exposed to this part watch intently.

Now everyone is convinced we are on the right path.

## 1.30 PM

Hot pizzas have made their way into the room. Hands reach out to grab a slice. You may have guessed that we are a foodie sort of team.

So, what exactly is the creative we are planning to carry into the meeting?

Phase 1: Questions Campaign: to run for three weeks, created for print and television.

Phase 2: Achievements Campaign: to run for two weeks, to be created in print.

Phase 3: Vision Campaign: to run for three weeks, to be created for print and television.

Additionally, an urban campaign to run for the entire duration till elections in English and Hindi weeklies, to be created in print.

I leave the room after three hours. The creative guys and Rupam get into a further huddle. Work gets divided and allocated. Which team will work on which Phase? It's a heavy headload. And it has to be created in three days flat. No real-time for iterations upon iterations or missing deadlines. Eye on the ball. For everyone.

Point to note is that most of our teams think and create in English. Now we have decided to present a regional approach. Therefore, all work should have a Hindi version at least. Sanjeev, our Hindi writer, is a competent guy with an affable air. He is bracing himself to partner Koustuv (Kosty) to do the writing.

Rupam comes to my room to say, 'The guys have returned to their workstations. We should see the first ideas and thumbnails by tomorrow evening. Time unknown. Whenever they are ready.'

'Sure,' I say. 'We all just need to remember we will have a day in hand post that.'

In an advertising agency, the thumbnail meeting is the first cut creative output. All feedback is taken, and the required changes are made. Sometimes if the work is off brief, it has to go back to the drawing board.

We don't have the luxury of not getting it right. Fingers crossed.

As the creative teams set off to work, I lean back on my leather chair. I listen to the news and flip channels. English,

Hindi, Vernacular. The television was set up in my room only when we started work on this project. One in my room. Another in the client service hall and a third in the creative department.

In all my 'free' time, I am absorbing the news. There is so much activity between political parties. Coalition planning, alignments, headquarters of the parties buzzing with movements. I do notice that the Congress party is low key.

I call in some of my other managers and staff and check with them on the other accounts of the agency. Spend the next few hours with all the teams who are not involved in the pitch. Things seem to be okay. *Thank god.* Life is chugging along fine in one direction at least. The teams working on the regular clients of the agency are having a hard time. A lot of agency resources and time are getting usurped by the Congress account due to the breadth of work required. However, they are managing to pull off their tasks professionally with positivity and a no-cribs attitude. The entire agency knows the criticality of this job for us. We are desperate for a win. All of us.

I must now get into a meeting with the finance head of the office, a young Chartered Accountant named Prince Khaneja. He is very thorough, diligent in his approach to work. Just the kind of person you need in a function like the accounts department. I have jumped the gun. I ask him to think about the contracts and letter of agreement in the event we win this pitch. How would he like to proceed?

Anita Nayyar buzzes me. She wants to discuss the media approach. I tell her I will walk across to her office which adjoins ours. Feeling relieved to have a change of scene, I enter the

Starcom office. She greets me warmly. I look around her room. It's pretty. Women and workplaces. Something nice about them. We talk about how life's coincidences have made our paths merge again. We first met at Lintas where I had worked for close to eighteen years and she joined the media arm of Lintas-Initiative media. Now I join Leo Burnett and she joins Starcom, our media partner, within a few weeks. We wonder if the stars have something special planned for us.

Daydreams done, we get down to brass tacks. While we have been asked to come with just a strategy, we all agreed on the fact that we will carry the full campaign. Thirty minutes is too little time–remember, the Vox Populi is four minutes. We agree she will strategise a media approach to dovetail into the overall plans and be ready to present if required.

We are going ahead with all tracks covered.

As I walk back from Starcom, I notice Ali in a serious meeting in the creative department. Talking to the teams on this pitch.

Life is getting so hectic and complicated. I hardly have time for anything apart from the frenetic tsunami of work. I make a quick call to my Ma in Mumbai. I tell her you have to bail me out. Please plan a trip to Delhi, I plead. I need some help to manage my home front and more than that to be with my pre-teen daughter Tarini. Ma gets it. She promises to make her bookings soon. If there is rock-solid support I have, it's my mother. She's been a role model to me, with her encyclopaedic knowledge and perfectionism.

The phone buzzes. It is Arvind, my boss in Mumbai. His opening line to me always is, 'Jayshree! What's happening?' I update him on everything. He has been calling and discussing this pitch. At times I bounce ideas off him. I definitely want Arvind to be at the pitch. I re-check with him if his schedule has been cleared for him to travel to Delhi on the 14th three days away. He tells me it's looking tough as he has to travel out of the country. *Goodness!* I tell him he should be here. He says I'm trying. But go right ahead. Have no worries. *Oh god!* I now have to prepare to face the unknown political arena without my boss.

I tell myself tomorrow is another day. Let's see what unfolds.

## PAST 11 PM

I go down in the lift. The lobby leads to the lonely open basement. It's pitch dark. I cross the compound and head to the car park. Gopal Das, my chauffeur, is asleep in the driver's seat. I knock on the window. He opens the door jolted out of deep sleep. I ask him if he's eaten, he nods. We drive through the deserted streets of Delhi, reach home quickly.

My mind is back in office. When I left, it was full. Almost like the morning. All lights on. People working, discussing, ideating, arguing. Enjoying. The advantages of a young and hungry team. Full of energy and passion.

As the curtains go down on another day, I count my little blessings.

## JANUARY 13, DAY BEFORE THE PITCH

The morning comes too soon. Barely awake, I switch on

the news. It seems there are new rules and regulations with regard to political campaigns. I make a mental note to check it out once I reach work. The usual routine of studying all the newspapers follows.

The Third Front prime moved by the Left is cobbling together a force to reckon with. While they will perhaps not have the numbers to win the elections and rule the country, they will corner a notable number of seats without aligning with either of the major parties pre-elections.

I take a few minutes to dress well and put on light make-up. I have figured out one truth in life. If you are comfortable and feel you are presenting the best version of yourself, your day somehow goes better. Hoping this truth holds up today, I leave for work.

As I reach, walk past the reception and say a quick hello to Madhu who's behind the reception counter and see the inevitable apples, I pause for a moment. Take out my badge to swipe the security code. It's very quiet. Some young executives are at work. I take a few minutes and chat with them, all the time taking in the pretty office with multiple colours and decor. Rajiv Saran, admin in charge, keeps it extremely well maintained.

I go to my room. It is large and smart, glass wall all around giving a view of the great outdoors. I glance outside and see a few creative people sipping tea on the balcony, engaged in fervent discussions.

I ask for the security guard to come to my room. He confirms that it was an all-nighter. Most people left at the crack of dawn.

I make a note to order special snacks and goodies for the team. Rajeev confirms he will surprise us with the best options within budget.

As the day cranks to a start, I see Ali walk into his room. He buzzes after a while, saying we must brainstorm on the presentation. He has a rough draft done.

Rupam comes over mid-morning. He says 'first cut' ideas should be ready post-lunch. The creative team is antsy. They need feedback and approvals. Very little time to go.

# CHAPTER 3

## BIGGEST PITCH OF THE YEAR

# THE PITCH IS TOMORROW

THE THIRTY-MINUTE slot at the meeting granted to us tomorrow needs to be orchestrated well. Every minute needs to work. My long experience of working with semi-government and government accounts at Lintas has taught me a few things. They are time conscious and thirty minutes would be just that. Usually, someone is assigned the task of ringing a bell and you have to pack up and exit.

Pitches get lost if the agency cannot complete what it wants to say. The degree of difficulty for us is that they have asked for a strategy. But we have decided to go beyond the brief. To carry Strategy, Creative and Media.

A rough division of time has to be made. My view is as follows:

- Two minutes for introduction of the agency team.
- Ten minutes for the strategy presentation, including quantitative research.
- Four minutes for the Vox Populi.
- Ten minutes for the creative work.
- Four minutes for the media plan.

For this to work with clockwork precision, every member of the team would need to practice and rehearse every last word. We already know we have very little time, perhaps none for a full-blown rehearsal.

We meet at noon to plan the approach. We decide to integrate strategy and creative into one seamless flow. Present the thinking followed by the four phases with the creative work. We decide one speaker will take it through as change of baton takes time. The mantle falls on Ali. He is a very competent presenter with an excellent command over both Hindi and English. He would be able to do justice to the job at hand.

A definitive learning I have from doing many many pitches in my career is that the agency team should be no more than six people. Large numbers are unwieldy. Also, I have learnt that each member of the team should have a role. If they don't, they should not be there.

The team that will go to the meeting is fixed: Rupam, Ali, Anita, myself and a couple of executives. The audio-visual equipment with a large screen and 29-inch TV are lined up. We have been given our time slot via a formal letter. Our time allocated is 5.30 pm, the last slot. Gives us two extra hours. Imagine if we were first at 2 pm. We would be leaving the office at 12.45!

But now it's back to the current time. We still have a day in hand, and we are still in the agency and the internal creative meeting is to happen.

Now the creative team troops into the agency conference room. This is usually a critical meeting. Everyone is attentive.

Kosty and Pooja present the first campaign. The question raising Phase 1. The anti-incumbency phase, if you like. The counter to India Shining.

He presents from the singular consumer point of view. Remember? To the '*Bus mein latakta hua aadmi*' brief nuanced by Arvind.

'Stock market *ne bade unchaiyan dekhi. Mujhe kya mila?*'
'*Woh kehte hai karodo nauri deen. Mujhe kya mila?*'
'Foreign exchange reserve *badh gaye. Mujhe kya mila?*'

Pooja has conceived this campaign in black and white. It's stark and real. The visuals are grim, representative of the common man's life. She has the maturity to know that this campaign has to reflect reality.

Kosty has paid attention to the slogan. He has written it from an individual's point of view. He has solidity in his writing style and stands very firm for what he believes in.

It's a powerful four-ad campaign. Designed to run as quarter-page newspaper ads in all major regional languages. For the moment conceived in Hindi.

We begin our discussions. Upfront, I tell them I like it. Ali also endorses it. We all do. It's perfectly dovetailing into the strategy we have outlined. Not only that, when you see something good, you just know it.

However, we debate if the ad should talk to individuals or club them under one umbrella of people not benefitting from the claims of India Shining. The common man for whom the forex reserves or stock market buoyancy was secondary to his day-to-day existence which had not got any better. In fact, as seen in the research, much worse.

So Kosty amends the line to 'Stock market *ne badi unchayian dekhi. Aam aadmi ko kya mila?*'

Thus, is born the slogan *'Aam aadmi ke saath'*. And the symbol of the Congress party being the hand gets integrated into the line. *'Congress ka haath aam aadmi ke saath'*. (The hand of Congress is with the common man.)

Kosty, Pooja and the rest of the team are happy with this development. They leave the room to go finish the campaign. They will also develop three television films and discuss the scripts later in the evening now that the direction is clear.

Another idea strikes in the process of brainstorming. Somehow all we seem to be doing is discussing the nuts and bolts of this issue. We talk about the gigantic budget being spent on India Shining, which seems excessive. When our findings have shown how many million Indians are starving and how many eat all their meals in less than one dollar daily. How a basic education does not reach all. How medical facilities need to be beefed up for the poor.

Why not do an ad on this aspect? In any war between two brands, there are strong issues put forth from both sides. Take the cola wars: Coke vs Pepsi. Car wars: Mercedes vs BMW. Mobile wars: Apple vs Samsung. Both parties are sharp. At the end of the day, I believe that consumers enjoy this debate the most. They learn. They laugh. They take sides and they watch out for the next advertisement, whichever side it may be from. And ultimately whoever they prefer.

We talk to the next team. Phase 2 of the plan. Achievements campaign. Another set of four black and white advertisements. To place firmly in front of the voter the real creator of most economic development in the country post India's independence.

There is one advertisement on each of these four subjects.

1 The Green Revolution.
2. The Industrial Revolution.
3. Upliftment of women to office-bearing roles in Panchayati Raj.
4. Introduction of technology and the computer age.

These are pretty straightforward. Each ad with a large visual and snappy copy. We know that only 3 per cent of people read long body copy. We don't want the ads to be dismissed as boring and passed over. Thus, the creative teams plan arresting visuals and just enough copy to make the pertinent points. This campaign is looking almost perfect at a thumbnail stage and approach. It's agreed upon with minor tweaks and the team is asked to finish it. Luckily this phase is just print ads. No films.

We decided to take a ten-minute breather. I head out past the client service hall and the creative department to the balcony. The air is crisp and cold. A few people from the office are scattered over the terrace. It's open and the most beautiful part of our office. Long, broad and L-shaped lined with tall eucalyptus trees overlooking the edge. Remember I told you we were in a *cul de sac*. I take some deep breaths. I have mentally fast-forwarded twenty hours and think of all of us heading to the meeting. So much to be done still. But an afternoon, evening, night and morning are four full-day segments left in our hands. Loads of time and yet not. No one on the team is cribbing or complaining. I think of how lucky I am.

The meeting begins again. Rajeev pops into the room to whisper to me that the evening snacks have come, the surprise he has planned. I say go ahead. Everyone in the office must get the treat. Soon some *chaat* from Chandni Chowk makes its way on platters. Much needed fuel to battle on. Yummy.

The next Phase is the Vision Campaign. Phase 3. The idea is to bring the consumer up to a point that he has heard the pertinent questions being raised, has revisited the Congress' achievements which have faded from his head and now is perhaps ready to ask: 'All very well. But what are your plans? Tell me about your plans. How do you expect me to decide to vote for you if you don't give me your vision if I vote you to power?'

So, a set of six advertisements in half-page colour size are being presented. The discussions begin. The switch from black and white to colour is to subtly connote better times ahead. This is what we are internally calling the Positive Campaign. Or the Vision Ahead Campaign. It sticks to the knitting of addressing the target groups. It promises them that their issues and problems would be addressed if they vote for a change. There are large-sized faces of real consumers and the hand symbol (which is the symbol of the party) is used. Each of them holding up their palm to confirm their allegiance. The creative teams use the hand symbol wherever possible.

Three film scripts are in development to sync with this phase of the campaign. Each film will cover one aspect. We zero in on Farmers, Unemployed Youth and Women.

The approach looks and feels right. This team also leaves to finish the final layouts. They return to the creative department.

It's going to take hours.

We also have to address the urban consumers. While our entire slant is to the population strata that is middle class and below, it would be wrong to absent the party from its loyalists in the urban areas. We come up with a plan.

Let's do an ambush campaign, we say, for the urban loyalist or fence sitter. A series of communications to run from the beginning to the end of the campaign period, irrespective of the phase of the campaign. Something like an underlying story unfolding every week.

We plan this for weekly magazines. Anita has joined in, she suggests *India Today* (English, Hindi and Telugu), *Outlook, The Week* (which is well circulated down south), *Femina* and *Women's Era*. A small list which would cater to urban consumers nicely. This campaign would run in double-spread colour print advertisements. The creative teams want to make this stylish and sophisticated yet powerful. No boastful rhetoric. Just straight, smart and hard-hitting.

Sounds good. Let's see what they come up with.

Marathon meeting over. It started at 2 pm. It's around 6 pm now.

We disperse. Each one heads off to their space. Prince, our finance head, is pacing outside my room.

He walks in even before I can sit down. He knows about this important meeting tomorrow and is reminding me I need to put in a 'terms and conditions' slide. We had talked about this earlier. We need to keep it simple.

Our last slide before the usual 'Thank You' one would be

simple and direct. It would say two things.

- All payments in cheque.
- All payments in advance.

Usually, this does not get put upfront in any pitch. But given that it's an organisation that doesn't do continuous advertising or deals with an agency regularly it's best to be upfront. I cringe. Feel awkward. After all, talking about money to strangers the very first time you are meeting is weird. But I quickly calculate. The flip side is even worse. Imagine beginning work and not knowing the financial way forward. And like everyone else, we too had heard horror stories of non-payments, cash collection in dribs and drabs in the past elections of multiple agencies and multiple parties. People making money through fair means and foul. No proof. Just hearsay. No one in particular. Just previous elections and the rumour mills that churned then.

Whoever knows me will tell you I will never play those types of games. I will be no part of this. Neither will my agency or my team.

Prince quickly runs through all the papers he has concerning the other business in the agency. He reminds me that we need to work on our projections for the year. Revenue and growth goals. Very soon all those MIS statements would need to be generated. I want to take an aggressive target. Aim for exponential growth. How?

I know this pitch will take up the better part of January. And if we don't win it, that's a full month gone. Even if the first round is mid-month, I am sure they will not decide on the basis of the first round. If we made it past the first round, there would be additional meetings and presentations. Life is never that easy. For starters, I don't know who from the client's side is at the meeting tomorrow.

I make a quick call to Shamim. Luckily, he picks up. Yes, Jayshreeji, he asks. Ok now, this is something I have to get used to. Jayshreeji. I ask him who will be there tomorrow. He says five or six people. *Hmmm* ok. Still don't know who.

Raju gets me my steaming black tea. I take a sip and call my comfort zone. Ma. She says she's wrapping up a few things and will plan her trip soon. Ma lives in Mumbai. She knows I am working late hours and riding on very little sleep. She tells me to be well clad and not catch a cold in the middle of this avalanche. Mothers! I am not sure if I can talk to her before the meeting tomorrow. So she wishes me well. As always, she says you will do very well. I smile and keep the phone down.

My thoughts drift to my father, no more in this world. The one who selected advertising as a career for me when I passed out of Jamnalal Bajaj Institute of Management two decades ago. While I was dithering with multiple offers during placement, he was the one who said, 'Take up your Lintas offer. It's a blue-chip company'.

Lintas taught me so much. It was the university of advertising. Thinking of my parents warms my heart. I have calmed down. And I am also happy to have joined Leo Burnett. It's a year. The most friendly, chilled-out vibe and an amazing focus on good creative work.

There's a knock on my door. Back to the present! Ali says he will share the presentation slides shortly. He also informs me the creatives will be ready in an hour to show the work in the next stage. This stage is when the approved thumbnails and discussions get put into actual layouts; representative pictures and the copy are put in the right size. Sanjiv is working with the English writers and they are co-creating the campaign in Hindi. So if an ad is a quarter page in a paper or half-page or double spread in a magazine—it will be created to the correct size.

Soon we are huddled around the laptop in Ali's room. While we have discussed the presentation, he has authored it very powerfully. For a thirty-minute presentation, we will have around forty slides, including the creative work. Roughly 35 seconds per slide and there is the Vox Populi tape with the actual research on it. Ali is a good presenter. Somebody else may have floundered. But he and I are confident he will deliver it on time without sounding rushed. While it has taken shape well, one thing we know is we will keep tweaking it till we leave for the meeting. Happens every time.

The part that needs work is the slogan and the rationale for it. It needs beefing up.

Now we head to the creative department. The work has to be seen on large monitors as it's a work in progress. At times changes are made then and there and we see it as the iterations go on. Rupam and team have taken a call to deglamorize the look and feel. To keep it very close to reality. To mirror the faces seen in the research. We were talking to people who were in the non-shining India.

Two hours are spent looking at each piece of work, and there's a ton of it. Remember?

Phase 1 - *Aam aadmi ko kya mila?*
Phase 2 - Congress *ke raaj mein hain humari sunvayi.*
Phase 3 - *Isliye main* Congress *ke saath hun.*
Phase 4 - Urban campaign. Change your life.

Pooja is hard at work, with her juniors pitching in. She has literally followed Rupam's direction of *Un-art-directed.* Every ad is looking stark. No fuss or frills. Real. No fake smiles. Kosty, Rupam, Ali, me, Kabir all are getting a feel in our gut that the creative work has translated the strategy on point. Totally on point. I am excited and convey this to the team. Now that they have a go-ahead, it's going to be a long night for them.

Ali and Rupam spend more time going through each ad in the presentation plan tomorrow.

Phase one, as I told you, now has a new line '*Aam aadmi ko kya mila?*' instead of '*Mujhe kya mila?*' This is sounding very very powerful and with the slogan '*Congress ka haath aam aadmi ke saath*', it makes a perfect marriage.

I walk back and Ali buzzes me an hour later on the intercom to say, let's deal with the changes on the presentation deck tomorrow. Fatigue has set in.

Yes! Best to look at it with fresh eyes.

In an eight-agency pitch, we have to be very careful that ideas and ads and strategic approach do not leak out. What happens is this. Every agency in its own way tries to do some informal espionage to get an idea of what the others are doing. Easy places to gauge this are from third-party suppliers. Translators and language studios, libraries for material, clipping services for research material. Editing studios outside your office. Which is why I was paranoid and had driven my team crazy to delete everything before they left. Someone in those offices can always be tapped for information. That gives an idea. The more dangerous sources of leaks are when someone inadvertently blurts out stuff to a friend from a rival agency. Somehow it always seems so innocent. You converse and then you realise you have blurted out something you should not have.

In this case, we make boundaries. We cordon off the team working on this client from the rest of the agency. It's like a secret mission. Computers are covered and discussions happen only when team members are present. The shredder is a very important tool all of a sudden!

Prantik Dutta, our head of Production services, has lined up exclusive studio computers and scanners for this job. No one is allowed to go to that area except the creative people working on this job. Prantik is a dynamic and energetic team player. Called Dada (older brother) in the agency, he is one of the most respected print and production experts in the city. His can-do attitude is an asset to any team.

I listen to the news in the room. It's silent and dark outside. In the agency, the atmosphere is electric. Everyone feels we have a very good package. A lot is riding on finishing it well.

Of course, a lot is riding on the vibe at the meeting too: how we can project our thinking and convince the decision makers.

I have finished for the day. It's been a long one. I choose to stay on a couple of hours for moral support, since everyone is still in office. Always feels good for members of the pitching team to have another shoulder to the wheel. I don't disturb them. They order food, perhaps a couple of beers.

I slip out of the office. Down three flights of stairs, through the scary basement to the comfort of my car. Just the headlights of the vehicle on the dark roads. Old Hindi songs on the deck and Gopal for company. He likes to chit chat. I ask him who he will vote for. He's secretive. But he voices a lot of issues, skirting around the answer.

## JANUARY 14

The big day is here. Somehow, being so wound up, I have slept poorly. I look at my face in the mirror, noticing dark circles. Make a mental note to use concealer.

Papers glanced at, TV blaring, I eat my breakfast quickly. I decide to wear a long black kurta and churidar. Team it up with a maroon dupatta from Jaipur. Jutties in maroon. A bindi. Dress to suit the client I am going to. For multinationals, it's trousers, shirt and a jacket.

We have decided to leave for the 5.30 pm meeting by 4 pm. No point getting stressed due to traffic delays.

I reach office early. The perils of presenting last are looming in front of me. The most obvious is that the client would be tired. Having heard seven agencies before us, what would be their mood and receptiveness level? Sometimes, if the timelines overshoot, some client members leave the meeting if they have other commitments. I tell myself I did the correct thing. We are not yet ready. And those extra hours are going to help.

Everything goes by in a tizzy all morning. We look at the presentation deck a million times. Check the Vox Populi a million times. Ali is rehearsing. As ads are completed, JPEGs are sent to him and he inserts the creative into the deck one by one.

Arvind could not make it but Pops KV Sridhar, National Creative Director, has come from Mumbai. He arrives in the morning.

Kabir calls Shamim around 3 pm. He confirms that the meetings are on in full swing. Delays are happening. I wonder if someone is that good and has got extra time.

We leave the office. Pops, Anita, Ali, Rupam and a couple of younger executives. A lot of people are yelling 'Best of luck'. 'Go kill' as we exit through the front door and wait at the lift lobby.

Well, it's finally happening.

# CHAPTER 4

## THE PITCH MEETING

# JANUARY 14

WE REACH LODHI estate. Many people are milling around. The presenting team is inside the annexe office. The rest are seated on chairs on the lawn and porch.

We take our seats and realise we will perhaps get our chance at 7 pm. Long wait. I also look around and realise I am the only woman there who is leading an agency. Such a man's world, this. *Ah,* but never mind. When I come to work, I don't think of myself as a woman. Just a person. It is people who put badges. And I have so much to say on this topic. For now, suffice to say: It's hard work to be treated as an equal. More about that later.

Some people find it hard to accept women in positions of authority. When I make eye contact with juniors who are men, some are shy, some sceptical and some plain arrogant. I can whiff these categories from far away. Wonder what these guys will be like. Soon I will know.

Paper plates with a samosa, a few chips and a sandwich are served to us. Hot masala tea, which is actually very good and uplifting. I glance around. The garden is expansive and pretty. Large dahlias are in bloom. It's getting chilly. Teams are waiting. There are still three presentations to go before we can get in.

What I do notice is that as the teams exit the annexe room,

they walk out of the long driveway without coming back where the rest of us are seated. We therefore have no clue of what is transpiring inside. I also notice they seem to be carrying a laptop, nothing else. Are they presenting from a laptop screen? If so, bad idea. How can 6-8 audience members peer into a small screen and give you attention? The screen limits you and puts a strain on them.

## 6.30 PM

The agency just before us has gone in. By now I notice for sure no one has brought equipment. So maybe they have it already set up in the room?

We are joking and smiling outwardly. Inwardly, shivering from more than just the cold.

It's 7 pm by the time we are told to go in. The first thing I see are paintings on the wall. There are 6 or 7 people inside including one man from a PR agency. All in white kurtas and shawls. Salman Khurshid is the only one we have met before. He says a polite hello. Ambika Soni, the only lady on the team, Ahmed Patel, Jairam Ramesh and senior Congressman and party treasurer Motilal Vora. They do look a bit tired. Not surprising considering the endless presentations they have listened to.

'Start!' we are told. Patience has probably run out. I tell them we would need five minutes to set up. Please give us that time. What setup, they are bewildered. Just start is the order again. It's late. I hold my ground. Very firmly, I say, 'We need to set up our screen and television. Our presentation needs to be seen like that, anything else would be suboptimal.' I say politely: 'Please do give us five minutes.'

They look baffled. I am now sure no other agency planned ahead and brought the equipment—large screen, *et al.* They must have assumed that they would go to a conference room with all these facilities available just like all the regular clients. So much for pre-planning.

Our guys are in and we all hurry to get going. Their guys get up and leave the room. Perhaps stretch their legs and breathe some cool air. Five minutes becomes 10 minutes before we are all set and seated. Ali is standing, he will present.

I thank them for the opportunity and introduce each team member with a line or two about their credentials. Also, myself. Tell them upfront we have carried the full package and gone beyond the brief. Don't know if it is making sense but they are listening intently. Basically, I reiterate that we are going to show you every ad.

Ali starts. He sets up the context. The situation in India. The competition. The consumer. Goes into the problem statement. What we are up against?

Now he enters the meat of the talk. Our thinking processes. Our defined target consumer. Our message. Our slogan. The four phases of the campaign.

Before showing the creative, he says, 'Let's bring the consumer to you. The Vox Populi will be played which has a cross-section of our research.'

The television screen springs to life and consumer upon target consumer (semi-urban and rural) appears in the room, literally, and says how their life has been *bekaar* in the last five years. How they have never heard of India Shining or Bharat Uday.

They are stunned. A group of weary people suddenly come to life. They look at each other and exchange excited glances.

Jairam Ramesh asks us as soon as the picture fades.

'Is this real?'

And before I know it, I am replying ' No. We held a gun to people's heads and made them say this.'

Of course, it was meant to be a joke. No one laughed. They don't know what to think of me, I am sure. But I am very clear. To me, this is a normal client. I am not going to be afraid or speak unnaturally. No one asks anything. I amplify and explain the process of research. How we sent out teams all over India. How we edited hours and hours of raw footage and that they are welcome to see all the footage if they want. They seem convinced.

Can we see it again they ask? It's played out again. Remember, I told you this was explosive stuff. Nothing like bringing in the potential consumer to the boardroom.

There is a change in their body language. They are excited to see the rest of the presentation. Twenty minutes are over and we have a ton to present. Here is what we present.

Phase 1: '*Aam aadmi ko kya mila?*'

"5 करोड़ रोज़गार देने का दावा."

आम आदमी को क्या मिला?

सद्भावना और विकास

पिछले 5 साल में केवल संगठित क्षेत्रों में 1 करोड़ 50 लाख रोज़गार कम हुए हैं. आइए, इस बार उसे चुनें जो नौजवानों के साथ है. कांग्रेस को वोट दीजिए.

कांग्रेस का हाथ आम आदमी के साथ

Unemployed Youth. The Government promised 50 million jobs. 'What did the common man get?'

"स्टॉक मार्केट ने नयी ऊँचाइयां देखीं."

## आम आदमी को क्या मिला?

सद्भावना और विकास

लाखों लोगों की मेहनत की कमाई किसान विकास-पत्र की बचत दर में कमी और यूटीआई घोटाले में डूब गयी. इसलिए आइए! इस बार उसे चुनें जो छोटे निवेशकों के साथ है. कांग्रेस को वोट दीजिए.

कांग्रेस का हाथ आम आदमी के साथ

Middle-class investors had lost lifetime earnings in scams.
Stock markets reached new highs. What did the common man get?

"किसानों के लिए विशेष योजनाओं का दावा।"

आम आदमी को क्या मिला?

सद्भावना
और विकास

ब्याज की दर, कर्ज का बोझ, सिंचाई की कमी और फसल
की सही कीमत न मिलने से हजारों किसानों को आत्महत्या करनी पड़ी.
इसलिए आइए, इस बार उसे चुनें जो किसान और खेत-मजदूर के साथ है.
कांग्रेस को वोट दें.

कांग्रेस का हाथ
आम आदमी के साथ

Issued by the All India Congress Committee (AICC), 24 Akbar Road, New Delhi 110 001.

Special schemes were announced for farmers.
What did the common man get?

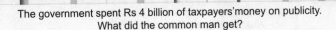

The government spent Rs 4 billion of taxpayers' money on publicity.
What did the common man get?

They ask a lot of questions. Our strategy of actually creating the ads and presenting them today has been a cracker of an idea. They have been able to see what is proposed, they don't have to imagine. The creative output is right there. Of course, with suggested pictures.

The meeting goes on for over an hour. They ask a lot of questions

Our slide with terms and conditions for advance payments by cheque is projected. No one says a word.

We start winding up quickly. They look a little more enthusiastic and exchange glances amongst themselves. They say we will revert. *Ah*, that usual mysterious line at the end of any pitch.

The one non-party man who works in a PR firm comes up to me and uses an officious tone. He demands to have a copy of the entire presentation deck. Send me the CD, he orders, handing over his business card. I am alert. And suspicious. Very early in my career, I have learnt not to share my thought process so easily. End of the day, that's our intellectual property, right? He demands it be sent the next morning. I murmur something incomprehensible. I realise none of the members of the client team are asking for it. I wonder if he is an external expert aiding them in the selection process, or just a hanger-on. I decide not to give it at all. Not unless I am told specifically. And anyway, before they take a decision, why would we give our material? After all, it's very easy to duplicate someone else's work and pass it off as your own.

We leave that house after what seems like ages and ages. As

we walk out of the driveway, Pops says let's go for a drink. The Claridge's hotel is nearby. We step into the bar. Post-meeting discussions are always interesting, fun. We are tired yet have a renewed lease of life post-meeting.

We discuss how they looked like a set of disengaged people at the start of the session. Almost defeated. Giving up before it's begun. But as the presentation took shape and by the time it ended, how the same people looked so charged up. The *piece d' resistance* was the Vox Populi and Customer Research. They saw people in their constituencies mouth so many problems live and saw how this set of people were disgruntled, angry.

With Pops proclaiming 'We are winning this!' we call it a night after a quick drink. We thank Pops for making it to Delhi and bid him goodbye. He is on a morning flight back.

Such a relief! Nothing to worry about on the work front tonight. Of course, much anticipation for the feedback and results call. When would it happen?

Bidding a very warm, full-of-thanks goodnight to my team, I head home.

After many days, we will all get home before midnight. It's just 10 pm.

# CHAPTER 5

## THE WAITING GAME

## THE NEXT DAY BREAKS BRIGHT. IT'S THE 15TH OF JANUARY.

I REACH THE office a little later than usual, deposit my bags in the room and head out to the wraparound terrace. I have figured out all the other agencies in this pitch. Some of them are fierce competitors. This is the most prestigious pitch in the Delhi market and the media is buzzing with it.

Finally, all members of the team are in. We sit together for a while, recollecting the events of the previous evening. People who had worked on the creative and research and all those who could not attend the meeting want a ball-by-ball commentary on how it went. What were the reactions? Pooja, Kosty, Creative teams, Sanjiv, Kabir, Amit, Vikram are all ears.

We are desperate for some feedback but want to come across as cool and nonchalant. Very casually, later in the day, someone makes a call to them. The results are not out.

I decide to keep watching the political news but focus on all the other clients of the agency. Go and meet with a couple of our existing clients. Send Arvind an SMS and update him on the meeting.

Somehow the day seems quiet, even dull after that frenzy of the last nine days. Much needed quiet.

The next day dawns. We get a call summoning us to South

Avenue. What could this be?

Seeing the 'war room' is like a reality check. It has a small space and an almost desolate look and feel. How were they going to fight the onslaught of a seemingly on-the-ball, aggressive opponent?

As you enter the premises, there is a small canteen. Two boys are in charge. They bring tea in cups and saucers with some nondescript biscuits.

We wait. Jairam Ramesh walks into the main meeting room. He wants a run-through of the entire campaign again. Salman Khurshid joins in. We flip open the laptop and present the slides. They question us on a lot of details, research design, creative approach and execution details if we are to work with them.

They ask us to enumerate our terms and conditions. I talk about two aspects: the usual rhetoric of advance payment and cheque mode. To which they always have a rejoinder: No leaks at all from your side. It will not be tolerated.

Then I explain there are some components to the agency payment structure. A commission from the media on each release which is between the media and the agency. And a production cost of shooting the pictures, artworks, illustrations, translations, photography, media release material like bromides and positives and such-like items which do not fall under the purview of a media release. By media release cost, I mean the advertising which appears on television, newspapers, magazines, radio and video on wheels etc. The amount the media charges to carry the ad or run it. So basically, two components of cost: Media and Production.

I realise they are not well versed in the nitty-gritty of dealing with an agency. But it seems to me they have figured out stuff and are double-checking. I play my cards upfront and straight. No other way.

This out of the way, Ali asks. What is the feedback? When will you decide? We get a short answer: 'We have not concluded. We will let you know.' Goodness. The plot keeps thickening.

On the way back, I am quiet, wondering what this meeting was all about. Obviously, we are in the running or they would not waste precious time. Rupam asks us if we noticed all the soft boards in the room with each state charted out. Much as we had done at the start!

*Another couple of days pass. It's now the 18th. We begin to think we may be out of the race. All quiet.*

And on the 19th, we get a call saying you need to come with the entire presentation. Renuka Chowdhury has come in from Hyderabad and they want to bounce it off her. Another day passes. Again, another call. Again, a trip to South Avenue. Bounce it off Digvijay Singh, who has come from Bhopal. Next day Mukul Wasnik. And so on and so forth.

We seem to be part of a never-ending presentation circus. Again, a difference. In the usual world of marketing, it's just the VP Marketing and CEO who takes a final call on agency selection. Here it seems the scope is wider. And getting wider daily.

Late nights, when I am returning home I usually message Arvind. One such day. I write to him: 'I don't know what's going on. We seem to be on a non-stop treadmill. Standing in the same place and running. Don't know what I'm doing with my life. It has been a fortnight and it is utter madness.'

Arvind writes back: 'You have my 100 per cent support.'

'We will let you know' is the usual answer whenever we ask the party if a decision has been taken. So, a week passes, and I wonder what the hurry was. It's now 21 January. We clearly don't understand why so much time is being taken. We are out of the race, is our thinking.

A call comes through a couple of days later. Jairam Ramesh is on the line: 'Please be prepared for Round 2 of the pitch.' Oh, so it's not over yet. Phew!

So, what is Round 2? How many agencies? All? Some shortlisted ones? It's difficult to tell.

We are given a date: 25 January. Morning at 10 am. Meeting at 10 Janpath. Oh! So, this is the big one.

We review everything we've got and make a few changes. I call Arvind and ask him to come for this meeting. He's back in India and readily agrees.

Through the rumour mills and some deft information gathering, we have figured out that it's just two agencies going into the final round. Six have been eliminated. We also know the other one is a small owner-driven agency, one that positions itself as a creative hot shop. *Hmm*. Interesting. As I said earlier, these are the hardest ones to read. What angle would they sell themselves on? Low cost? Speed? Best creative? Difficult to gauge.

I decide to focus on our strengths. Medium-sized therefore fast. Young and energetic team. Passionate. And by now all key members are clued into the political scenario. We have learnt fast. We have learnt well.

The day before the meeting, we are informed to be well in time. My number is at the gate of 10 Janpath. The names of members from the agency team have to be logged in with them for security reasons. No one but people with those names will be able to enter. We give them the names of our team. Again, crisp and small. Seven people in total. All representing a function or role. We also give in the names of the equipment supplier. The 35-mm television screen and sound system will accompany us. We dare not fiddle with walls there and are not sure of the conference room facilities or what sort of place we will present in. No chances will be taken.

We do a full-blown rehearsal in the agency.

We disperse with a plan to meet at 10 Janpath at 9 am. The meeting is at 10 am. We are also in the know that about fifteen people are attending this meeting. Nervous tension is building up.

# CHAPTER 6

## THE MEETING AT 10 JANPATH

# JANUARY 25

I OPT FOR a nice salwar kameez. Add a jacket, shawl and put on a small bindi. All dark colours.

It's damn cold outside. Misty and freezing. The type of weather where your breath comes out like smoke when you exhale.

I tell Gopal 10 Janpath. He double-checks: 'The house next to the Congress headquarters?' I say yes. I am lost in thought, mentally planning the meeting and thinking of questions they may raise. How to counter those? I am also wondering who those 15 people attending the meeting are. Also, a bit nervous, honestly speaking.

My phone beeps continuously, a series of text messages have invaded my inbox. Each member of our team on reaching or nearing is updating their whereabouts. Suddenly I look up and see that I have reached close to New Delhi Railway Station. It's already 9 am. I exasperatedly ask Gopal where the hell he thinks he's going. Looks like he is more nervous than me. He is lost and I'm terrible with directions. Why today of all days? Now we are turning around and getting into the circular *bhool bhulaiya*s of New Delhi. Arvind has reached 10 Janpath. He calls me 'Jayshree where are you?'

Like most advertising people, I deftly skirt the issue, saying, 'Just reaching.'

After a nerve-wracking time and what seems like ages, I somehow make it. It's 9.20 am. What's daunting is the crowded reception area. Clearances demanded as at airport security. I get a pass and put my bag, jacket and shawl through the scanner. I emerge on the other side and scan the grounds. I walk straight and see the office-like structure adjoining the house. Many people are at the door. I walk to the entrance and spot Ghulam Nabi Azad, Pranab Mukherjee, K Natwar Singh, Ambika Soni, Kamal Nath and so many more faces I have thus far seen only on the television news.

The agency team is still outside. We still haven't gone in to set up! Why? I'm sure once these people are seated, they would not appreciate being kept waiting. We see Ahmed Patel talking to someone. We request him to let us in, explaining a setup time is needed. Screen setup. Sound setup, TV setup, booting the laptop.

Finally, a man in a security uniform wearing a trench coat beckons to us. '*Aap log andar ja sakte hain*' (You can go inside.) It's now 9.40 am.

The meeting will start at 10 am. We are sure of that, as so many bigwigs have arrived already.

Arvind is insistent on knowing where I went early morning. Why was I late? He smiles while he asks. I tell them the New Delhi station misadventure. All the time everyone is quick at work, unzipping laptop bags and setting up the hardware. Ali places the laptop on a table. The officious security guard proceeds to give us a dressing down. He literally scares us. 'This is Indira Gandhi's writing table! Don't directly put things on it.'

Err, ok, we didn't know. It's the table facing the really large oval table. Around 25-30 people can sit around it, that large. Note to self: It's a lovely piece of furniture. There is a drawing room-like seating area in the same room with sofas and large chairs. The sofa is a minty green.

Ali says in frustration: 'I think I'll hold the laptop and present.' All of us break into nervous laughter.

Meanwhile, Mr Officious Trenchcoat comes to take the status. He says, *'Jo aadmi bolega woh andar rahega, baki sab bahar jao.'* (Only the one who is presenting will stay inside, the rest of you go outside.) Goodness. What the hell is that? So, we are supposed to line up and wait outside while our own meeting is on? This takes the cake and bakery.

Ahmed Patel comes into the room. Clearly, he is the convenor of this meeting at 10 Janpath. *'Kyun bhai? Aap log ka hua ki nahin?'* (Have you people finished?) We say we are ready. Just that this gentleman wants us all out. Quickly, he sorts that out. We survive. Looks like we can attend our own presentation!

He is told we are ready but need approval to place the laptop somewhere. The buzzing voices outside in the meeting room annexe are getting louder. Looks like everyone is here.

He organises a cover for the table. The laptop now has a perch. It's seven minutes to ten. The main doors open. All the senior Congress party leaders walk in. While I'm not taking names, suffice to say the room was filled with erstwhile ministers and future ministers: Dr Manmohan Singh, Mr Pranab Mukherjee and so many senior leaders. Of course, the team we had presented to in the first round was there. Except for the PR man. *Hmm*, I always knew he was a hanger-on.

The seat at the head of the table is empty. The door at the far end of the room opens. There is a hushed silence. Sonia Gandhi, President of the Congress Parliamentary Party, has arrived. She takes her seat. Her party people greet her. I notice how smart she looks. Maroon saree. Black jacket. Hair short with the ends turned up.

She looks up at us and in faintly accented English says, 'Good morning.' Ali is standing diagonally opposite them, the rest of us are seated on the sofa. I stand up. Thank them formally for their time and the invitation to present. Introduce my team. Arvind steps in and takes a couple of minutes to talk about the agency credentials. Now it's over to Ali, who is the best man for the job given his proficiency in both Hindi and English.

Twenty sets of client's eyes are on him. He is always a competent presenter. But today he brings on his A-game.

Strategy context set up.

Problem definition made.

Approach listed out.

Consumer research shared.

Vox Populi played.

The consumer enters the boardroom.

Same gasp all around the table.

*Aam aadmi ko kya mila?*

Congress *ka haath aam aadmi ke saath.*

Four phases of the campaign listed:

Questions.

Achievements.

Vision Ambush.

Media dispensation on TV and print.

Rebuttals if required.

All ads presented in Hindi and regional languages.

English is just 10 per cent.

Regional Blue Ocean strategy reiterated.

Now the last slide.

Terms and Conditions.

Presentation ends.

It's on the dot of 29 minutes, one minute ahead of schedule.

Like any place where passion is rife, where belief is entrenched and where strategy meets creativity, our presentation cuts like a hot knife through butter.

All the time, my eyes are swinging between the slides up on the screen and the research presentation and the heavyweights of the party taking it all in. I note their body language.

It's intense. Attentive. No one looks at their phone or talks to the next person. There is pindrop silence.

Once it ends, Mrs Gandhi turns to her team and asks

them if they have questions. A couple of gentlemen raise some points. Dr Manmohan Singh and Pranab Mukherjee also ask questions. Those get duly answered and noted.

Arvind says he wants to make a point. He brings up the issue of leadership. It's a pertinent point. He says, 'AB Vajpayee is clearly the announced leader of the NDA. His popularity is at an all-time high. There is no candidate announced from your party.' There is silence in the room.

In his own way, Arvind conveys that a friendly empathetic face would have to be projected. Right now, she has had very little public-facing interaction. She listens. Does not say a word. But does not react adversely.

The meeting is declared over. Mrs Gandhi politely thanks us for our efforts and says we will revert.

We pack up and leave. As we head out, I see the second agency waiting. Their team also has 6-7 members. The two partners are all set. I am acquainted with one of the two: we wave out and I wish him luck.

Energies are drained after that adrenaline rush. But we are feeling very good this morning. After twenty days from the day of the first call, we know we have done the very best we could have.

Everyone back in the office wants to know how it went. When will we get to know? Over cups of hot tea, coffee and soup, there is an animated recounting of all our new experiences. And, of course, the thirty minutes when we were centrestage.

Now begins that desperate phase of waiting for the decision. Time is running out for them: Elections are around the corner. Formal dates have to be announced. The other agency, a small one, fancies itself as a creative hub. Sometimes these alternatives can prove to be dangerous as it's difficult to predict their approach.

A couple of days after Republic Day, it is afternoon. The sun pours in through the glass windows of my room and I relive the events of the month for the hundredth time. I have two major worries. If we lose this pitch, we have also lost a precious month in what I have defined for myself as a crunch year. My second worry is that if we win this pitch, how will we cope. The scope of the assignment at our end is huge. Would it be possible to pull it off?

The phone rings and brings me back to the present.

It is one of the joint owners of the rival agency. The one I know like an acquaintance. We exchange pleasantries. He says he has a plan and wants to discuss it with me. I say, 'Go ahead.' He says, 'Why don't we meet?' I reply, 'Let's talk on the phone'.

This is his idea. 'Why don't we go together to the powers at INC and say we will jointly handle this campaign? You guys do television and we will do the rest.' Clearly, he knows the weakness of his agency, what it cannot handle. And thinks he understands our strength. And our weakness. I am immediately put off. And I rely heavily on my first instincts in life. Not liking this cloak and dagger approach.

He has a complete plan as to how we could deploy this scheme and throws a very persuasive line about how both will win if we are agreed on this. 'Chances are,' he says, 'they will appoint one. We are smaller and cheaper and therefore our chances of winning are very strong,' he proclaims. A bell goes off in my head. Really? So why are you making this plan? Nevertheless, my mind is racing. We need to win this pitch like our lives depend on it. All the mad work of the last 25 days flashes before my eyes. We are almost in February and have had no wins so far because all our energies were locked in this effort. Should I? Something would be better than nothing. I have an entire team outside my office room looking to me for solutions. What should I do? If I got at least a part of this business, we would be comfortably off.

However, sharing our ideas? An absolute no-no. Giving someone a chance to run away with our thinking? No!

Taking a deep breath, I refuse point-blank. No amount of fearful debate with him or my own mind budges me. I do not tell anyone about this call immediately.

I tell him, 'Let's wait it out! It's all or nothing. Let's take the risk. And if there is to be a division of responsibility then let the client decide and say so. I am definitely not going to prompt them.'

We are confident of pulling off a full-service solution. TV, newspapers, magazines, radio, video on wheels, posters, stickers, collaterals, multiple languages and everything it takes. Once it comes, if it does, we will find a way.

Big risk. But I took it.

A couple of days later, the client called. We are asked to come to the war room for a meeting. They want a discussion! What would the verdict be? As we sit in a modest room sipping tea from small cups sent from the makeshift kitchen, we are given the news.

We have won the pitch. All of it.

I reiterate our terms. By now they are tired of hearing about mode of payment, I guess. We are given some strictures from their side.

They would like to know how we will keep the confidentiality of the operation from beginning to end. The previous campaigns have led to ads being leaked out before release, giving the opposition enough time to plan rebuttals and place it in the newspaper on the same day. They definitely do not want a repeat of such slipshod, clumsy work.

I assure them we will put in checks and balances. They repeat this again and tell us firmly it will not be tolerated at all. And that we should share our plans on this issue with them very quickly.

Overarching financial terms are discussed. I tell them we will work on agency commission for media releases and give them a production rate card in advance for non-media work.

Most importantly, I say, 'We need a formal letter from you appointing us. We would not be in a position to do your work without a letter followed up by a formal agreement.' All this is a bit alien to them. The last month of working with them has taught us that the political world is a verbal world. It's more speak than write. It works that way. But we cannot compromise on this part.

'Ok, we will get a letter organised. Please start work.'

## FEBRUARY 3

So much to do. So little time.

We are driving back to the agency. We have told them not

to announce the result in the media till we give them a plan of the work way. The confidential way. Just did not want to be inundated with media calls and interview pressures till our internal plans are in place. They agree.

Back at my table, I have mixed feelings. Very happy about winning perhaps the biggest pitch in the Delhi market for 2004. For sure. Beating seven agencies. Working relentlessly. Taking risks.

Very fearful too. Feels like the weight of the world is on my head. Now having made the promises to INC, we have to pull off this gigantic job, already running late, nothing begun yet.

My mind talks to me. It tells me to shut up. It says you're halfway done. You guys have a brilliant strategy. Go ahead, execute it.

My mother's voice rings in my head. 'Don't be mediocre' is her mantra. Come first or come last. Just don't be one of those teeming millions in the middle. Okay Ma.

While my room is quiet, and I am having mental debates, outside there is euphoria. Winning this pitch is sending a giant wave, an adrenaline rush roaring down the agency. There are happy faces, smiles, and excitement in the air.

Rajeev Saran comes to say he is ordering hot jalebis. 'We must celebrate.' By now you must have noticed: our treats are always yummy but utterly cheap cost-wise. Of course, I agree.

I make a call to Arvind. He says I have had no doubt, since I attended that meeting at 10 Janpath. He tells me he will revert with some plans. He is also excited.

Post-lunch session the same day.

All department heads are in a meeting.

Ali - Account Management

Rupam - Creative

Prantik - Production Services

Prince - Finance

Anita also joins us. As you know, she is heading our media partner Starcom.

Six of us now sit together to make a work process flow for this client. Very different from the others. With each day and each move being tracked by journalists and the competitive pressures being high, the onus for confidentiality lies squarely with us.

The overriding things we discuss apart from many many tiny details not being enumerated here are as follows:

1. Make a core team. No one on that team is to discuss anything with anyone. Except the members assigned to this job. And by that, we mean even friends and family outside the office.

   Just no one. It's always tempting to discuss your work with your loved ones. Or to show off about it at times. Or to share ideas. But that's not happening this time. All of us are totally agreed on this. Younger team members, studio artists and even office messenger boys would have to buy into this plan. One cannot enforce this. It's your personal code of conduct. But everyone's word would have to be taken.

2. We also decide to deploy stricter rules for entry and exit from the office.

3. The main decision taken is to build an extra room in the office. The engine room, as I call it. Where the computers, scanners and printers for this account would be. Four studio artists are dedicated to this job. A shredder would be dedicated to this space. The machines we use for this work will not be deployed for any other account. This is the room where the work would be executed and readied for media release. We also plan to put a notice outside saying Limited Entry. And put the names of the people allowed to enter.

4. We decide to get a new set of cellphones for each member of the team. A phone on which calls for this account will be made. No other calls would be allowed.

5. We agree to add additional security guards.

6. Two additional shredders are to be bought. One for the secret room and one near my office. Every extra piece of paper is to be destroyed.

7. Media. Now we also realise a lot of work with external vendors will happen for sure. Media is one of them. When ads get produced finally, they are converted to positives and bromides. This gets couriered to newspaper offices all over the country. It gets received at a newspaper office and set into the pages for print. Similarly, for television, there are so many processes of approvals. At an initial stage, scripts have to be approved by the channel. Only when the approval comes do we

shoot the film. So, all possible loopholes to be plugged in this arena.

8. Another major area is translations. Usually, agencies have in-house English writers. Luckily, we have a Hindi writer too. All language translations usually go to the language shop. These are places which work for all ad agencies. They offer services of translators in all Indian languages.

   Given that our campaign is going to run in multiple Indian languages per release, we wonder how to fix this critical aspect.

   Let's ponder on that.

9. We decide to give the client and its rival code names. Never refer to them as Congress. Now we have fun deciding the code names.

   We choose common surnames from Delhi: Khanna and Mehra. One for Congress the other for BJP.

10. Lots of systems and procedures for the Finance department. We need to fix advance payment methods. Collect advances well in time before external suppliers get paid. One thing I am clear on: We would only do the job and pay out money after collecting it from the client. This is a huge challenge. Prince makes a note of everything. He says he will consult Harish, who heads Finance in Mumbai and is his boss.

    Yes, we need all the best brains in the agency to collaborate and advise. I am a great believer in being inclusive.

11. There is also the issue of Film Shoots and Radio Production. The best talent for all that work is in Mumbai. We make a note to keep draft Non-disclosure Agreements for partners, vendors and supplier's photographers and filmmakers.

12. Back to translations. We decide to get the work done in-house. Our Mumbai office has a number of translators coming in daily. There is a language department there. Languages not available could be sourced from third-party experts. This is a huge area for potential leaks. We decide to take this off the Delhi radar screen.

A dedicated fax machine is set up for this in my office area. An account management executive in the Mumbai office is assigned this job. A fax machine is dedicated to this work there. When the Hindi or English copy matter would leave the Delhi office, Jasbir would call the executive who would place himself at the machine. He would pick up the paper and go to the translator and get it done. Fax the translation and call Jasbir who would stand by the machine and drop it off at the secret room. The original would be destroyed in the Mumbai office. This is the level we plan details to.

This process planning meeting goes on for hours and hours. We have decided to stop and convene again the next morning.

It's past midnight. My cellphone buzzes.

It's a call from the Congress client. Yes! All kinds of timings for calls! Again, a difference from other clients. Early mornings, late nights! As it is with them—always straight to the point.

'You have to be at 10 Janpath at 11 am.'

I sit up straight. *Whoa*! *What's this now?* I thought things were settled. Are we opening up matters again? I am told, 'You have to meet them.' Who is Them? And I am told no one from the team dealing with us will be there. Mrs Gandhi would be there, of course. Now I am totally confused.

Anyway, hardly able to get proper sleep, I send messages to Ali, Rupam and Anita apprising them of this development. It's 7 am. All of them are now in the same boat, questioning the why and what of this meeting.

We leave well in time. Definitely don't want to be late for a meeting with Madam. Clearing security and walking through the grounds reminds me of the pitch day. The entrance outside 10 Janpath is like a large cavern. There are a number of desks and people manning them. All your details have to be given. My name is registered there along with the number.

We reach the door of the anteroom. Unlike the other day, no one is there. A secretary comes to tell us we can go in. Back to that room!

As we enter at the head of the table much like the other day is Mrs. Sonia Gandhi. We are greeted by her with a sense of recognition. She is cordial. Next to her are Rahul and Priyanka. Ok. I finally get it. They are Them.

What happens next is rather sweet. We get seated opposite them on that large oval table. The mater does the introductions. She says, 'This is Priyanka, and this is Rahul,' and I am chuckling to myself thinking who doesn't know them. But I find it so gracious on her part not to make assumptions. I, in turn quickly introduce the team we have brought to the meeting.

Priyanka looks a little under the weather. Looks like she has a cold. Her mother asks her in Hindi: '*Kya hua?*' Again, a surprise. Then she tells one of them: '*Kamra se mera ainak le ke aao.*'

That being out of the way, she offers us coffee. You must have guessed our response by now: the always eating-drinking gang. It's also super cold temperature-wise and we are super tense inside too. Of course, we are trying to not show it.

Now Mrs Gandhi asks, 'I hope you have the presentation you made to us the other day.' We say yes, of course. She says, 'Please repeat it. I would like to hear it in detail once again'.

Three sets of eyes are on the slides. On the phases. On the slogan. On the Vox Populi research. On the creative approach. On the media approach.

Over the next two hours, they ask a lot of questions. Rahul in particular gets into the details of the research. The respondent profiles, sampling methodology, etc. Both quantitative and qualitative.

Priyanka asks questions on the creative.

They seem to like the slogan: *Congress ka haath aam aadmi ka saath.*

They also find merit in the Vox Populi leading to *Aam aadmi ko kya mila?*

Priyanka asks us to do some radio spots along with the campaign thought. Yes. Very much on the cards but not created yet. In an election campaign where the target audience for us is rural and semi-urban, radio as a medium would play a huge role. Especially for farmers.

Coffee gets served. I notice the cups and saucers: slim, tallish cups in pristine white with matching white saucers. The coffee is filtered, delicious. Not the usual machine coffee.

They are polite. They see the plans end to end. Make a few comments and changes. Mostly visual. Sizes of huts. Look of fields. Farmers. Faces of Dalits. I realise we are talking to people who have been into villages and district interiors of the country much more than any of us.

For example, we had put in a picture of what we thought was a small hut depicting a destitute Dalit home. They correct us. They say a home this size would be a landowner's. You have to get the right picture. Must change it.

Taking all the feedback and ending the meeting thereafter, we gather all our stuff and prepare to leave. 'Thank you,' they say as we exit.

Now we are walking back past security to the grounds outside. Call for the car and wonder if the meeting met its objective. As a meeting, it was cordial and polite, and the campaign seemed well received. I definitely felt Mrs Gandhi seeing it for herself almost privately was getting herself familiar with the details. She seemed to have bought into it fully now.

That's the sense we get. But will have to wait for a call from Jairam Ramesh or Salman Khurshid to give us the feedback.

At office there are a series of people waiting to meet me. Prince Khaneja, our Finance head. A smart young CA in his first stint in an advertising agency. I had hired him in August. He has been around for six months. A good team player. Fortunately, a common resource between us and our media partner.

He literally enters my room along with me. He informs me that he has had a long chat with Harish, our agency Finance head in Mumbai. They have created certain financial structures for this account. Harish wants to come down to Delhi and spend a day, discussing details. He says this is very important. Of course, I agree. I tell Prince to book Anita's time too and request him to come over as soon as possible.

Prantik has some more ideas on production processes with the external vendors: printing presses and makers of positives and bromides. What we had discussed yesterday was internal studio functions within the agency, easier to manage than outsiders. Also, potential easy leak areas. How many people who are not your own can you control? He plans to make backward arrangements with each press he will use for confidentiality. Separate machines. Cordoned off areas. Work at night. Which means the press would have to be kept open for us.

Prantik Dutta is a man with good connections and respect in the printing world. He is affable, energetic and a wonderful team player, as mentioned earlier.

Rajeev Saran is next in line. He has talked to a contractor to build the secret room. He shares first estimates with me. I tell him to reduce it by half. He stares back in exasperation. I say ok, 60 per cent, no more. He exits.

I order tea and a few biscuits. I am a typical Bengali that way. 'Cha biskoot' gives me comfort. I sit quietly and dunk each biscuit in hot sugary tea, take a three-minute break.

Now that the sugar rush has entered my system, I feel

energised. But I wonder why no call has come in from my day-to-day client contacts of the Congress party: Ramesh or Khurshid.

## FEBRUARY 4

We had said the first phase of the campaign needs to start mid-February. India Shining is pelting away. Now I notice as I read those papers at home and office that most PSUs and Government ads have the 'India Shining' tag on them. Lots of media pressure. Everywhere you look, you see it.

Meeting a deadline of release in ten days is looking impossible. So many ads to shoot. So many translations to do, so much production work and media deadlines.

There is no formal letter as yet. There is no agreed budget. How are we to begin?

I am very clear I will not start without either.

So the waiting game begins.

As they say, there is many a slip twixt the cup and the lip.

And I am hoping we don't fall between the cracks.

Anything can happen.

## FEBRUARY 6

The thirteenth Lok Sabha has been dissolved and poll dates are likely to be announced shortly. Prime Minister AB Vajpayee met with President Abdul Kalam to recommend dissolution of the House on January 27. This was after completing the constitutional requirement of the passing of votes-on-account. With the dissolution of the 13th Lok Sabha eight months ahead of schedule, the stage is set to elect 543 members of the Lower House of Parliament.

As I said earlier, there was a lot of media support for the ruling party. Typifying this sentiment are extracts below:

> With the Lok Sabha to be dissolved in the first week of February, what appeared to be a tiny wave in August 2003 seems to have crystallised into a tsunami. The country's most exhaustive election tracker, the INDIA TODAY-ORG MARG Mood of the Nation Poll predicts 330-340 seats for the NDA, almost 30 seats more than the 304 it attained in 1999. Accompanying the saffron surge is its mirror image, a slide for the Congress and allies, with the poll predicting 105-115 seats, 30 less than its tally in the last elections...
>
> *—India Today issue dated February 9, 2004*

And there is also this:

> While Vajpayee's popularity ratings have soared to 47 per cent, that of Sonia remains as low as 23 per cent, a far cry from the December 1998 INDIA TODAY ORG-MARG opinion poll, when her popularity, at 31, was higher than Vajpayee's, at 27. Arguably, popularity ratings matter more in presidential polls than parliamentary elections but with Indian elections acquiring the vim and vigour of US-style elections, the Congress is in serious trouble with its present leader.
>
> *—India Today issue dated February 9, 2004*

Magazine covers, February 2004.

The days are now whizzing past very quickly. There are endless rounds of iterations and fixing and refixing the creative work. There are detailed meetings for the media strategy which include both media planning, media buying and media scheduling. Motilal Vora is taking the lead on this part, particularly the media buying and scheduling aspects. Jairam Ramesh is present in these meetings looking into the media plans. Anita Nayyar is leading from the Starcom perspective. Once the media list is finalised, each media house for the print medium and each TV company are being met individually, turn by turn, for negotiations on rates, positions of ads and other term finalisations.

# CHAPTER 7

## THE DYING AND RESCUING OF THE CAMPAIGN

# FEBRUARY 7, TEATIME

WE ARE BACK at 10 Janpath for a meeting, mainly to discuss the budget. Today, Mrs Gandhi is not presiding over this meeting. Voraji, Ramesh, Rahul and a few others from their side and our team are present. The budget we have presented is a minuscule fraction of what the main competitor is spending —whether you go by the official figure of Rs 80 crore or the unofficial figure of Rs 300 crore.

What we proposed is cut down to less than half in this meeting!

There is a deep sense of helplessness in the agency team. How are so many phases of the campaign and all the plans to be translated into action with a minuscule budget?

Major debates begin around the table.

We keep insisting and reiterating that this is a bare-bones budget, and could they please find the funds to translate the approved strategy into reality.

Apparently, it is not possible.

Now begins a heart-breaking process. Can we cut the first Phase? Should we do away with the urban campaign? Should we reduce the number of advertisements of the vision campaign from five to three?

Everyone in the room is giving suggestions, butchering the plan slowly but surely.

Voices are getting animated and passions are running high. I'm trying my best to control my temper, which seems to be slowly raising its head. So far, I am succeeding but just about. If we cut and chop and change, the proposed strategy will not hold good. This is the worst nightmare of any agency. That too, at a time when all the work is approved and it has taken us a month to get to this place! Looks like in one fell swoop it's all going to crumble. There is only one result of an activity such as this watered down, less impactful plan: Sure failure.

As I watch, I see a decision veering towards cutting off Phase 1 of the campaign, *Aam aadmi ko kya mila*? I brace myself to take on the fight. Under no circumstances am I going to allow this to happen. According to me, this is the most powerful entry point to counter the wave of India Shining. Without it, we are almost benign. Without shouting, I raise my voice to a pitch that makes everyone sit up and takes notice. I am usually not the type that talks non-stop. So, everyone gives me a moment and listens. I look them straight in the eye and say firmly that this part of the campaign is going to give the slogan teeth. It is the most potent.

The question being raised, *Aam aadmi ko kya mila* is the headline thought, leading to the sign-off: Congress *ka haath aam aadmi ke saath*. The public would have a catchphrase to counter all the catchphrases created by the BJP. And we cannot afford to drop this Phase of the campaign at all.

In my mind, this part of the campaign has been created to counter phrases with massive currency like 'feel good factor' and 'India Shining'.... And to give them the platform to take the fight ahead in Advertising, PR, roadshows and rallies.

India Shining (*Lekin*) *Aam aadmi ko kya mila?* (India is shining but what did the common man get?) This is the connection that we want Indians to make. Those Indians in the unserved markets, as I said earlier. In my mind, this phrase will be the much-needed talking point.

Rahul looks at his team. He says, 'I think she has a point on Phase 1. We should keep it.'

The meeting is inconclusive. Lots of heated debate and passionate questions. Nothing firm. We are fighting hard to keep the plan intact. But the budget is still less than half. Voraji says, 'Let me revert with a final figure tomorrow'.

Now, this is leading to a major problem. Without agreements on the spends, I am reluctant to take a letter from them and there is no sign of their preparing it either.

## FEBRUARY 8

We are told the budget is up by another couple of crores. At best, it is just half the amount we have proposed. This would mean the following:

Cutting newspapers and magazines and TV ads by half.

Cutting campaigns down from 4 ads to 2 ads.

Everything truncated. Watered down.

Should we drop a phase? We believe the only Phase that can be dropped is Phase 2: Congress achievements.

I wonder how to convince them. How can you be heard with no money? What are we doing?

It's all very disappointing.

Next day, there is a scheduled meeting with Priyanka. The radio scripts are ready. She had taken a keen interest in wanting to hear them and had brainstormed ideas in our previous meeting.

At this meeting, after hearing the creative she asks if we have started work. What is the progress? Will we see the ads soon? When are they releasing?

I tell her there nothing has started. As we are in a quandary of cutting ads and phases. She is very clear.

She has a quiet aggression about her. She looks at us and her team members. She says, 'It's all or nothing' She repeats. 'All or nothing'

A voice speaks up. I realise it's mine. I say equally firmly. 'It's all or nothing.'

Now that's a huge risk. But I know this was a bare minimum and the output would be very weak if we cut and chopped and chipped and made a mish-mash plan. Later we will get blamed for poor performance of an invisible campaign.

She says, 'Leave it with me. We will give you the Go/No Go decision tomorrow morning.'

No Go? No Go?

Everyone is quiet. 'Fine,' we say.

My team agrees with me fully. They endorse my stand. The hours that follow are excruciatingly tense.

I tell everyone to suspend work for this client. To chill and go home early.

Arvind calls. I relate the saga to him. He figures I am upset.

He reiterates: 'You have my 100 per cent support'.

## FEBRUARY 9, 10 AM

We get a call from them. And lo and behold, simply put: The Budget has been fully approved. Not one paisa cut.

I wonder what had transpired from when we left. Some major moving and shaking must have taken place.

Anyway, it has finally happened.

'Start straight away.'

'Where's the letter,' I say?

## FEBRUARY 10

By now my mother has arrived from Mumbai. So has my sister from the USA. They have hardly seen me in all this time.

We are out for dinner. Need to spend some time with the family too.

My phone beeps. The family looks at me in frustration as I bend my head to check the message.

It's Ali from the AICC headquarters. He writes just one line.

*Letter received.*

I finally break into a huge smile. My family wonders what just happened. I call Ali. I want to know all the details. He says Voraji was baffled about this obsession on our part about the formal letter. So, Ali tells him with his brand of humour which Voraji is slowly getting exposed to, 'Sir *jab tak tambu nahin lagega shaadi kaise hogi'* (Sir till the tent is not constructed how will the wedding happen?)

## FEBRUARY 11

A bright new morning. The weather has got milder. The sun is yellow and not watery.

Even before I reach office, I message Jasbir to organise a meeting with the entire team. I also message Arvind Sharma requesting him for time. This is not something which I want to break to him over a text message.

The conference room is full. Extra chairs have been put up to seat around 12 people around the table. The rest are seated in a second line. This is the team on the Congress client.

News about the letter finally coming in is only known to Ali, Prince and me. The meeting begins. We wish each other. I don't beat around the bush. It's been over a month. These guys need some good news. Desperately. Everyone has been tense and worried. I break the news to them.

We have WON the pitch. Fully. No division of work. They want a one-stop shop. We have it. We will give it to them.

There is so much happiness and joy in the room. Thrill. Validation. Excitement. Clapping. High Fives. Young faces all smiling. Looking at this sight is enough to justify the hard work and lack of sleep of the past five weeks.

Once young members feel ten feet tall, the world seems invincible. After all, many of them are below 25. And will be catapulted onto the big stage without going through the usual struggle. I am confident we will manage, though this is going to be a challenge.

I make a motivational speech. Reiterate how awesome everyone is. Because it's true and I genuinely believe it. I recount all our hard work. Since we are all together, I bring them up to scratch on all the stuff that has happened these last few weeks.

Rupam and Ali also brief them about the entire run-up.

Now we ask them to roll up their sleeves and be prepared for a hard journey ahead. The best part of being young is to have so much to learn and look forward to. Also, together there is combined energy and an aura of safety in the comfort of our office.

# CHAPTER 8

## IMPOSSIBLE DEADLINES

# FEBRUARY 11

DREAMS OF BREAKING the campaign on the 15th are just that: dreams.

Before we start scrambling to our workstations and smaller breakout groups, I have to underline the importance of confidentiality. How there cannot be a single leak. Of course, no one would do it on purpose. But absolutely no carelessness. No loose talk. No telling anyone anything. Around the table one by one we all take a pledge.

First things first. We need the advance cheque for Phase 1. Ali and Prince take this on. Two days is all they have to raise estimates and collect a chunk of money. Not for us. For onward transmission to the media, both print and television have made an open declaration that they will NOT release any ad without advance payment. For any party. No credit days for anyone. Therefore, the media release order which authorises the publishing of the ad will go with the exact amount it costs by cheque. So now that the media has this dictate and it's splashed all over the news, it makes our life a little easy.

It's not like we are making a fuss. Everyone seems to be protecting their finances. Why has this taken so much precedence? Large sums of money get spent in a short time period. Usually, clients have credit periods with an agency. Sometimes 30 days, sometimes 21 days. It all depends on the Letter of Agreement that gets signed. But what has been observed with past elections is defaults after losing the election or non-payments, a big issue.

If Phase 1 cannot release on February 15 then what's the earliest date we can? Four 100 cc black and white ads. But all need to be shot. The three films. Need to be shot in Mumbai. All to be done in eleven languages. Final sign-offs still required.

Everyone exits the room. On my way back, the TSM trainees ask to meet me. All 14 of them troop into my room. It's their last day. The first, most meaningful relationship I have with them is being their professor. I ask them how their experience was in the real working world, feeling guilty all the time about not giving them enough time. They all talk at the same time. Assure me they have learnt a lot. Feel sad to leave. Bright-eyed. Looking at the future happily.

The ones who worked on the pitch want to know the result: Did we get the account or not? I say we will know in a few days. There! My practice of non-disclosure has begun. I find myself a little partial to the young girls in the group. Ask them to stay back.

I begin to give them my two bits of advice. About work-life balance. About conducting life in the office. About being damn good at your work so that no one can question you. About making things easy for yourself so that you can work at peace. By that, I mean keeping the domestic infrastructure solid. You are earning. Pay salaries. Uplift other women. Don't get into physical chores. Conserve energy to use it in the workplace.

I now look outside my part-frosted part-glass door. I see shadows. People are waiting. Say a warm goodbye to the young ladies. They file out.

We have been summoned to South Avenue. The media plans are running into countless newspapers state wise. The client has approved this plan and doesn't want to cut out any publication. Starcom has given a cost sheet for the approved plan that has blown up the budget. Voraji and his team want to do full justice to each state. As in an election, it is imperative to reach everyone 18+. A creative solution has to be found. A smaller size campaign is created in the lines of the main four ads. For district and rural papers. Where even a 60 column-centimetre ad would get noticed given that the clutter levels are low. Anita, of course, will try and ensure page 3 or 5 top-of-column position given the clout of her agency.

Phase 1: '*Aam aadmi ko kya mila?*' That's what we are working on today.

| The Unemployed Youth |
| The Farmers |
| The Middle-class investors |
| Women |

We create a 5-ad small version of this campaign and work on the messagess.

| A farmer's wife |
| A suffering mother |
| A poor Dalit |
| Jobless youth |
| Ladies affected by scams |

उन्होंने मेरे परिवार का क़त्ल
मेरी आँखों के सामने कर दिया
और पुलिस कहती है कि
कुछ नहीं हुआ.

धर्म और जात-पांत के नाम पर अत्याचार करने वाली इस
केन्द्र सरकार को अब मैं बदलूंगी. कांग्रेस को वापस लाऊंगी.

कांग्रेस का हाथ
आम आदमी के साथ

Issued by the All India Congress Committee (AICC), 24 Akbar Road, New Delhi-110 001.

They killed my family in front of my eyes.
But the police say nothing happened. (Referring to the Gujarat riots)

मौजूदा केन्द्र सरकार से
आम आदमी को क्या मिला?

मेरे बेटे ने देश के लिए जान दी
और उन्होंने
देश की इज़्ज़त ही नीलाम कर दी.

कफन घोटाला तक करनेवालों को मैं कभी माफ़ नहीं कर
सकती. मुझे इस घोटाला सरकार को बदलना है. मुझे कांग्रेस
को वापस लाना है.

कांग्रेस का हाथ
आम आदमी के साथ

Issued by the All India Congress Committee (AICC), 24 Akbar Road, New Delhi-110 001.

My son laid down his life for the country but they destroyed the country's self-
respect. (Referring to the scam involving imported coffins for soldiers killed in
Kargil.) What did the common man get?

मौजूदा केन्द्र सरकार से
आम आदमी को क्या मिला?

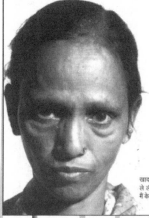

जब मेरे पति ने आत्महत्या की,
तो परिवार के 8 लोगों की
सारी ज़िम्मेदारी मुझ पर आ गयी।

खाद के बढ़े दाम और लोन की बढ़ी दरों ने मेरे पति की जान
ले ली. जो हो गया उसे तो मैं नहीं बदल सकती पर इस बार
मैं केन्द्र सरकार बदलूंगी. कांग्रेस को वापस लाऊँगी.

कांग्रेस का हाथ
आम आदमी के साथ

Issued by the All India Congress Committee (AICC), 24 Akbar Road, New Delhi-110 001.

Responsibility of my 8-member family fell on me when my husband committed
suicide. (Referring to farmer suicides)
What did the common man get?

मौजूदा केन्द्र सरकार से
आम आदमी को क्या मिला?

सरकारी गोदाम तो अनाज से भरे हैं,
लेकिन ग़रीब का बच्चा भूखा सोता है।

मैं अपने बच्चे को भूख से तड़पते अब और नहीं देख सकता.
मैं इस हालत को बदलूंगा, कांग्रेस को वापस लाऊँगा.

कांग्रेस का हाथ
आम आदमी के साथ

Issued by the All India Congress Committee (AICC), 24 Akbar Road, New Delhi-110 001.

Government godowns are full of foodgrains.
But the poor man's child goes to sleep hungry. What did the common man get?

45 years of my husband's savings vanished in 45 minutes.
(referring to US-64 financial scam). What did the common man get?

We go to South Avenue.

The ever-helpful canteen boy has started recognising us. By now he knows our preferences. Rupam drinks coffee, Anita and Ali normal tea, me black tea, etc. We get served with a smile.

The place has got a bit active. In the far room at the back, there is activity. Some computers have been placed. A few young people are sitting behind monitors.

Congress lineup: Salman K, Jairam R, Ambika S and M Vora.

Agency lineup: Rupam, Kosty, Pooja, Anita, Ali and me.

We take them through the dilemma. Can't spend most of the budget in Phase 1 given that so many newspapers have been added. Yet we do realise it is of utmost importance to reach every potential consumer.

We forcefully recommend the strategy of four quarter-page ads for semi-urban areas and a set of smaller ads, five in number, for the rural papers. We are sure it would make the impact we want.

In the fifteen days of this phase of the campaign the consumer would see an ad every four days in urban centres and every alternate day in rural papers. Along with television, this would be potent.

They see the merit in the recommendation. They review the proposed creative. It is rough work at this stage churned very quickly to give an idea. In principle, they are fine with it. But get into details of the subject of each ad. Scams. Unemployment. Farmer's widow's woes. Middle-class woes. In other words, the unserved market's woes.

मौजूदा केन्द्र सरकार से
आम आदमी को क्या मिला?

5 साल में 5 करोड़ रोज़गार का वादा,
लेकिन दिखा एक भी नहीं.

एम्प्लॉयमेंट एक्सचेंज के चक्कर लगाते-लगाते मेरे जूते पिस
गए. अब मैं अपनी किस्मत बदलूंगा, कांग्रेस को वापस लाऊंगा.

कांग्रेस का हाथ
आम आदमी के साथ

Issued by the All India Congress Committee (AICC), 24 Akbar Road, New Delhi-110 001.

They claimed they would create 50 million jobs in 5 years,
but I haven't seen even one.
What did the common man get?

A full campaign is created over the next twenty-four hours.

While the five small ad campaign is being developed, the creatives come out with a nice hanger to present the thought. The same line of thought.

'*Maujooda kendra sarkar se aam aadmi ko kya mila?*'

Strong visual. Minimal copy which makes the point and the slogan. 'Congress *ka haath aam aadmi ke saath.*'

Before we go back to present this, we create the ad which we have ideated on in the car. A very noticeable ad is created with a little girl holding up a placard which says—With all the money being spent on advertising so many hospitals schools, tube wells etc. could have been developed. '*Aam aadmi ko kya mila?*'

This is an unplanned, undiscussed addition. We decide to take it along.

Another marathon meeting starts. Everything gets discussed threadbare.

We tell them we are starting the production process. We need to plan the still photography and film shoot.

One thing we realise is that they have no archives of photographs. Nothing. Unlike most 'normal' clients who maintain archives with their agency or within their offices.

With normal clients, there is no such fear and terror of espionage and leaks. Most agencies use photobanks like Dinodia in Mumbai. There is no question of sourcing the photobanks at Delhi or Mumbai or even other cities. Word gets around. Not just competitors, even the media. That cannot happen. Lots of times perfect images can be bought for a fee from photobanks. That option is ruled out.

Everything has to be originally shot! For each picture, we need to keep backups ready. There is no gap to go back and reshoot as time is very very short. Now the campaign in Phase 1 is four large ads and five small ads totalling nine ads. All to be released in eleven languages each. That's 181 ads of original work. Multiplied by 250+ newspapers. Now imagine these ads going to 250+ newspapers, all scheduled according to issues in that particular state, metro, non-metro, etc. each time a release takes place. That's the mind-boggling, mind-bending level of detailing—humongous is the word.

Rupam has a lot on his plate. He, fortunately, is a talented photographer himself. He mentally decides to take his camera along from now on. In case he needs to shoot something and cannot find the right photographer.

It's mid-February now. Lots of work ahead. The month is short. I was in Mumbai the day after we got the letter, for a workshop. Something I could not get out of. Coffee break, the lunch break and tea break to meet three potential ad film producers. All top-notch and all professional.

They have driven out to the Powai hotel I am staying at which is the venue of the workshop. Of course, at different time slots. Lunch break. Tea break. Post-session. I verbally brief them on the films. One by one. Without giving away the script entirely. Ask their willingness and availability. All are keen. Very keen. After all, it's a different genre of films from the usual and a prestigious project for them.

They are all interested and available and can definitely add cinematic value. I decide to hand over envelopes with the scripts to three of them.

And anyway, for audit purposes we need three competing quotes.

The Farmer's Wife. A 20-second powerful film with her sitting in her hut and talking about the suicide of her husband. And about how she is committed to bringing a change. Her eyes are ablaze, and she looks angry yet determined. The Super appears. *Kisan ko kya mila - Aam aadmi ko kya mila?*

The Unemployed Youth. A 20-second film. With an unemployed youth sitting in a decrepit verandah, throwing little stones into the air with controlled anger. With each stone he chucks, he mouths his anger of being jobless and of seeing no employment. Despite promises.

The old man who has lost his lifetime's savings. Sitting in his little home. Talking of his dreams of making his son an engineer fade before his eyes. And how he will bring change. Angry. Sad. Yet determined to cast his vote.

I also apprise them of the confidentiality of this project and that absolute care will have to be taken there is no scope for anyone to know. I tell all three to revert with costs and a note of how they will ensure my concerns. I'm worried. Editing studios. Sound studios. Film shoots with a crew. Even a simple, innocent casual conversation can lead to the spread of information. It's normal to say 'I can't meet you today, have to edit those Congress films' or 'Am busy. Will call later. Doing music tracks or recording voice-overs for those Congress films.'

Such conversations can't happen.

This is the stage till when our creation is safe with us, in the safe haven of the agency. Now it needs to go out to get executed. Trust everyone, JMS, I tell myself. There is no other way. If you are anxious, they are too. End of the day, you are picking the best partners you possibly can.

KS Chakravarty (Chax) gets selected to make the first set of films. His office sends in a competitive quote and creative-wise his showreel is brilliant. There is a high level of comfort with him as our Mumbai office uses him a lot.

Kosty is in charge of this project. Ali accompanies him to Mumbai for the shoot.

It's the 17th of February. No one could have moved faster than this.

While it's lights-camera-action frenzy in Mumbai, far away it's madness at Delhi. Media plans for Phase 1 are being finalised. Hours and hours are being spent with television channels and newspaper and magazine representatives. They are trying their best to secure the best contract for their companies and Anita and the Starcom team negotiating very hard to get rock-bottom rates. Voraji is personally attending all these sessions. One morning at South Avenue, the war room, while Anita, Ravi and others are in media negotiations, I am discussing other issues in the front chamber. I see Teena Singh of the *Times of India*. Apart from knowing her professionally, we are good personal friends too. She is attending the meetings with Starcom. She tells me it is a herculean job at the newspaper's end too, with so many back-to-back releases and metro and upcountry edition deadlines. Upcountry editions go into print earlier than the metro edition. So, if we delay sending the ad in time, the upcountry edition does not carry the ad. It has to be rescheduled and given that there are nine ads there is a lot of detailing and micromanagement required.

Most days these negotiations start early mornings and go well past midnight. There's a small tea stall outside the office. To take much-needed breaks, Anita and her colleagues walk down for a cup from time to time.

The media sheets per state look endless. What this means is that once the ad is ready, tons and tons of positives would be couriered overnight across the country. Different languages. We were also choosing subjects of ads depending on the issues in the state. So it was a very complex matrix.

State: Tamil Nadu. Language: Tamil. *Daily Thanthi* xyz ads. *Dinamalar* xyz ads. So on and so forth.

Starcom has media veteran Arun Soni in charge of this operation. He does not hand over or delegate. He keeps his eye on the ball. He has long nights ahead of him. We fix backward contracts and non-disclosure agreement clauses with the courier guys.

Now as the print ads go into shooting, I realise there will be a non-stop series of them. Nine ads over 15-20 days. That's like a lot of work, given each would be multiplied by language. The kind of work large clients would do over half a year.

Usually, translations are approved by the client. Of course, we need their approvals. So they need to be told about these procedures. Sure, they say. Bengali will be approved by Pranab Mukherjee. Gujarati by Ahmed Patel, Gurmukhi by Dr MMS, Urdu by Shamim or Salman Khurshid, Hindi by Janardan

Dwivedi and such names on the list. Usually, young account management executives run around and get these approvals and normally this task rests with middle-level executives at the client's end. The process involves showing the original copy in English or Hindi and the language translation.

Now we have a new worry. How will things happen on time with busy, senior people assigned to this task? My point is they too are not delegating. Everything is being held closely. How to approach these people?

I decided to implement a system I was used to working on in my earlier agency. A label at the back of each final artwork. With each and everyone in the process to sign. Art director. Copywriter. Creative Director. Account Executive. Head of Account Management. Head of Production. Media Buying Executive. Client.

Everyone agrees this is a good plan. Somehow this is that insight that once you put your signature on things, you are that much more careful. Once the client has understood that this is standard operating procedure, they comply quickly. Salman Khurshid is the person who will be the one point of contact on this. The client signatory for all creatives.

The more pairs of eyes, the less the chances of mistakes. But working through this massive list of people is going to be a challenge. The onus is on the account executives: Kabir, Amit, Vikram. I make a note to myself. Haven't these guys, 22-23 years old, grown 10 feet tall? Amazingly responsible and accountable as each day goes by.

In the far distance, I see Prantik has just returned from

the press to the agency. He has a mammoth task ahead. Night upon night of producing material for release. Somehow, he manages to remain calm while carrying such a huge workload.

Rupam decides to shoot authentic pictures in villages. He has made a creative strategy for this campaign. He discusses it with his team and all of us.

He calls this approach '*Un-art-directed*' creative, as I have mentioned earlier.

So, while India Shining is very art directed—perfect families, happy people, loads of bright colours—this will be the reality. Real faces. Stark. Honest. Truthful. Nothing 'addy'. He also has a process in mind for the post-production of pictures.

Rupam is one of the best art people in the country. He has done some amazing campaigns in his career. This too is an example of how he is true to the task at hand.

He enlists photographer Pankaj Arora. Pankaj is quick, talented and young. Having worked in the agency before, with his own company, he is almost like an extension of the creative department.

Work frenzy is at its zenith.

- Still shoots in villages.
- Film shoots in studios and outdoors in Mumbai.
- Translations going back and forth on those secret fax machines between our Delhi and Mumbai offices.
- Translations being approved by the who's who of the party.
- Our executives running around late nights to wait somewhere or the other and get it done.

- Media plans being done and redone.
- Rates getting finalised.
- Labels being signed.
- Salman Khurshid being contacted to approve and sign off ads.

And before we know it—because no one knows how the time passed in that whirlwind, we find it's 22nd February. And it's 10 pm.

## FEBRUARY 22, 10 PM

And we are at 10 Janpath to show the final Phase 1 ads and films. Shot and ready for release. While most of India is winding down and ready to put the shutters on another day, there can be no such agenda where we are. Really tense and hoping for a 100 per cent approval so that we can meet the March 1 deadline. In my heart of hearts, I brace myself for changes. Every client does it. Fingers crossed there aren't too many changes, we hope.

We are waiting for Sonia Gandhi. She has been on long rallies covering many villages and districts in a day. That day she has been in Haryana. We are told she's just returned, will join us shortly. Jairam Ramesh is present as are six of us from the agency team. As a normal practice, we don't carry extra baggage.

Madam enters the room looking like she's had a long day. She greets us and we quickly get down to work.

We start with the nine ads of the newspaper campaign. Mind you, no newspaper would see all nine. They would be planned according to the city or town or village as per the issues there. But at least 6-7 insertions per paper for sure. An ad every three days.

Fortunately, we have planned for contingencies. Since it's majorly visual and mostly faces, we have shot backups of two to three faces per advertisement. We are carrying those alternatives to the meeting. Sure enough, two of the faces used for the smaller strip ads don't meet with approval. But as soon as Rupam whips out the alternatives, selections take place. So much for forward planning. And it's not easy to shoot so much extra. But it comes good! Phew!

But there are issues with the hut in one of the pictures. Soniaji explains it's too big. Not appropriate for what we are trying to depict. We promise to change it by reshooting and sending it back in a day or two for approval.

## 11 PM

The print campaign has been cleared with very few changes. That's a relief. Now massive execution and duplication are all that is required before it reaches the consumer.

Time to play the films. The TV and sound system have accompanied us to this meeting. There is a hushed silence. There are three films.

Unemployed youth. It's shown thrice. Hard-hitting. Well-acted. Crisp, to the point. They like it. It's approved. Like the rest of the campaign, it's black and white. No colour.

The second film goes on. It's the farmer's wife. Widow. Talking about how her husband took his life one night leaving her alone. Set in a hut. With her seated on the floor. Again, well-acted. Hard-hitting. Crisp. Black and white. However, the producer has used a tint and it is not exactly black and white in all its starkness. Her saree catches flecks of the red filter which is part colour, and this is not approved by them. They want it in pure black and white given that she is a widow. Any amount of discussion on creativity and filters is not cutting ice.

Things get a little tense.

Now comes the third film. The old man lamenting about not being able to make his son an engineer as he has lost his life-long savings in a scam. This film is in the order of the others. Same black and white. Stark. This film gets bounced by them. Totally. Just when I thought we were going back with few changes.

The saree filter resulting in colour flecks was worrying me. I was wondering how many days or what it would take to rectify it. But this was another level. Totally rejection of a full film was seriously scary. Why? They did not approve of the old man. They said it looks like he is reading from a script: looking down and reading. Now the back and forth arguments begin. We say no, no. He has spectacles so you may have got that impression. But they won't budge. There is no closure, at night, because we leave still trying to convince them.

It's past midnight. We are in the car park at 10 Janpath. Jairam says you will have to make these changes. Print, we agree. Saree filter. Fine. Can be checked with Chax. Reshooting a full film? Well…tough. And, somehow, we do not feel he was reading. It's left open-ended and we all head off in different directions to those rarely seen places we call home. It's dark and still. I have some western classical music playing on the stereo. Trying to relax. Can't seem to.

My mind tells me to look at things positively. At least nine press ads and one film are approved. And the image of the hut on the print ad and some other minor tweaking would be easier to handle. All local and in and around Delhi, and our internal studio. Rupam has understood what he needs to act on immediately. Am sure his mind is buzzing with it.

Ali calls me from his car. We vent on the old man film. Are they being too fussy? The rest of the observations and objections are justified, he says. He is planning to work on those issues asap. What about a bounced film?

Making changes is never easy. But in the client-agency world, this is par for the course—anything to make the work perfect. End of the day, the client is footing the bill. Sigh!

There is clearly a disagreement between them and us on the old man reading. We feel he isn't, they feel he is. Both sides argue. Put points forth. Night-time presentations. Something quiet about them. At least no one is angry and yelling. Mrs Gandhi, I have figured, speaks to the point. There is an economy to her words, and you have to get what she means. She never belabours a point or talks in an insulting tone.

None of us present in that meeting sleeps well that night. From 6.30 am, messages are going back and forth. I am lost in thought, drinking my special tea, a blend of Assam and Darjeeling. Flavour and body. The fourteen papers are piled up in front of me. It's 7 am. I wonder what the day will bring.

The ring of the phone pierces through the air on my balcony. It's Jairam Ramesh. He goes straight to the point using a very official tone.

Change the hut.
Change the saree.
Change the old man.

'And we want to see it tonight.'

I reply.

'Even God cannot do it.'

There is a silence on the line.

Why?

Because shooting a film in Mumbai, finding a crew, editing the film, laying a music track, approval of a model, post-production and finally a Digi beta tape getting readied and someone flying with it to Delhi cannot happen in a few hours when the producer does not know till now that he has to do it. In my heart of hearts, I am also worried they might not be free to take this on and have not started some other project.

More silence.

Then he says, 'So let me know when you people can do it.'

*Wow.* The day has begun with a red-hot ball of stress.

I, of course call Ali and Rupam. It's 7.15 am. The tension is rife. The producer's office is called. Kosty's ticket to Mumbai is booked. He is rushing on the first flight out. Our film producer partner fortunately understands the client and the odds we are up against. Not the usual. Not at all the usual.

He says, 'I shot the film. He was not reading. The spectacles are creating that illusion.' But he knows it's non-negotiable.

He swings into action. Gets another three models by noon. We get approvals. The film is shot in the afternoon. Evening and all-night editing music and post-production details are managed. Including colour correcting the filter on the saree. Kosty boards the first flight in the morning. We are at 10 Janpath by noon. All concerned people are present. Mrs Gandhi and the team of Salman Khurshid, Jairam Ramesh, Ambika Soni, Ahmed Patel and Voraji approve the films and the changed hut.

Phase 1 is ready finally!

## FEBRUARY 24

Three days to the release of Phase 1. Now there's utter frenzy in the agency. In-house production of artworks in multiple languages is brimming over in the secret room. The media team is receiving bromides and positives in heaps. Everything has to be streamlined and couriered out in time. To remote places.

Television channels are lined up all over the country. The Election Commission has banned political party advertisements. Congress supporters decide to release the campaign. It's not released as a political ad. It is being released in Public Interest with a message.

# CHAPTER 9

## COMMON MAN'S DAY OUT

# MARCH 1

THE CAMPAIGN BREAKS nationally.

Of course, without full-page ads and long TV commercials, it slowly slips in. Because of good media relations and the fantastic negotiations Anita and team have done, the ads are positioned prominently on right-hand side pages on page 3 or 5. Being starkly black and white, they stand out. The visual dominates and the line questions '*Aam aadmi ko kya mila?*'

And just like the movies, it is a 'sleeper hit'. What do I mean by this? It gains credence and word of mouth at the end of the first week. People are beginning to notice it. Slow and steady, it is making its myriad points.

The consumer has started noticing it. The message begins resonating. We do dipstick research to check on this and more than anything else it is the party rank and file who are reporting excitement and enthusiasm from the tiniest villages to the metros.

'*Aam aadmi ko kya mila?*'

Now the media has also taken notice. Firstly, they are thick on the trail of finding out who the agency is. They are shocked that they did not get a whiff of it before such a campaign with relentless ads was released. And we have covered this well with a decoy act: getting them to announce that the work is happening out of Bangalore.

The snooty crowds in urban centres are mocking the campaign: 'Have you seen what the Congress has released?' 'Some black and white stuff,' they sneer.

It's never easy to take feedback which is not good. A truism of life. However, we are sticking to our guns. Because that snotty urban consumer who in all likelihood will not go to vote is not our target consumer.

As I said earlier, our target consumer is '*Bus mein latakta hua aadmi*' and not the people who drive around in cars in cities.

Once Phase 1 is eight days into release, we do many quick telephonic interviews and take feedback on the campaign. It's starting to get noticed.

More than anything it is the Congress party people who are in touch with the ground realities, down to small towns and villages, who report positive feedback.

So far so good.

But preparations are on for Phase 2 of the campaign, which has a working title of being a Bridge campaign between the Questions Phase and the Vision Phase.

This is the four-ad Achievements campaign, due to run pan-India with a greater focus on regional languages. Again, modest in size. Black and white advertisements.

Now, this part of the campaign could have been in colour. However, colour ads usually have a 100 per cent premium in terms of rates. And we are on a shoestring budget. Remember?

The four subjects chosen as achievement of Congress rule are:

-Empowerment of Women

-Technology Revolution

-Industrial Revolution

-Green Revolution

-White Revolution

These ads are being designed and placed before the consumer to jog the memory of forgotten facts and truths. It's like signing in the muster all over again. Or placing your visiting card in front of someone who may have forgotten vital details about you. It's about reintroduction.

- Women empowerment speaks on the jobs created for women under Panchayati Raj. Where even Dalit and Adivasi women were given a chance. Women came into positions of authority in villages, and jobs were created for them.

- In the technology revolution, the consumer was re-acquainted with the fact that computers were brought in and disseminated during Rajiv Gandhi's regime. Putting a telephone in every village via the PCO so that everyone could be connected. Lots of jobs getting created as a result.

- Similarly, the Industrial revolution is speaking about the space programme, steel, urea and oil industries. Building of Public Sector Undertakings and giving loads of employment to backward classes amongst others, while encouraging the small-scale sector too.

- The Green Revolution, which brought self-reliance

for farmers. Schemes for them. Building of dams and irrigation.
- The White Revolution. Milk schemes. Making milk easily available to all.

Now, these four ads had to be shot. Rupam and Pankaj do detailed planning. They have to head out to villages and shoot pictures.

All four subjects get shot to represent the copy. It is integrated very well by Pooja in the art department. She has been working relentlessly.

Rupam has a hard time during this shoot. While he gets half his shots on the first day, when he returns to the village the next day, he is literally chased out. Everyone is scared, confine to their homes. He hears someone has threatened the people of this village not to participate in this particular shoot. Wonder who they were.

These are the vagaries of political advertising.

Ali and his team take a meeting at the South Avenue apartment. The war room is now buzzing with activity. The ads are shown in a corner of the room where only Jairam and Salman can see them. They are quite satisfied. Retain the final layouts for a quick dash to 10 Janpath where Madam will see them and approve.

The approvals come in that evening. A couple of copy changes and we are set for release.

The first Phase of the campaign 'Aam aadmi ko kya mila?' is at its tail end. It's March 18.

Phase 2 or the Achievements campaign will take over from March 20 and run till the 30th.

Now begins the rigmarole of internal processing. A tornado of activity.

- Same frenzy with multi-language translations via the confidential fax machines to Mumbai and back.
- Same running around by our executives Kabir, Amit and Vikram to get translations approved by party bigwigs.
- Any changes suggested go back via the secret process to Mumbai. Gets done there. Returns. Again, is taken personally to the powers-that-be to in the Congress party to approve and sign. Backbreaking, fatiguing process. But like every experience of life, the more you do something the more you learn. So, everyone in the chain of work learns by now that no delays are possible. No fuss. No attitude. Just quick turnarounds.
- The secret room is churning out language artworks by dozens and Prantik and Vijayji are going crazy getting everyone to sign the labels at the back of the studio artwork. People are screaming: 'Do I do my work or sit around signing?'

But nothing will be released without every signature in place. My rule. And it can't be broken.

So, while everyone is busy signing creative layouts, I am busy signing cheques. Remember, I told you the media was not accepting any political ads without advance payment cheques.

So, each release order to the media publication has the usual positives and progressives but also a cheque attached. This is another difference between regular clients and a political election-time client.

I am signing hundreds of cheques a day before any advertisement release. Wherever I am. Returning tired from a meeting. Heaps of cheques arrive on my table. Eating dinner at home. Cheques arrive with a rider.

Actually, my signing hand is protesting. But I don't complain. I mean it's the accounts department which is making the cheques, writing each one out. And approaching me with a sweet smile. We have this conversation where nothing gets said. Just gestures. Cheques are waved at me. I wave and say ok.

So, it looks like we are all signing cheques, media release orders, Translations and Artworks. So much so that when Salman Khurshid sees us from a distance and is busy elsewhere, he gets up and comes to our area in the war room. Asks: 'Anything for me to sign?'

Phase 1 of the campaign has seen no mistakes. No leaks. Keeping my fingers crossed. We need to sustain this. Everyone has to remain motivated.

# CHAPTER 10

## ACHIEVEMENTS

# MARCH 20

THE COLD IS abating. I am ready for work. It's still early and I have a light shawl on my shoulders. I am mostly in Indian clothes these days. Never know when meetings will happen. I lift the pile of newspapers. Haven't missed a day of glancing at them. I open the papers to see that the Achievements campaign has broken.

Each and every paper has carried the women's empowerment advertisement. About women being put in positions of power in the Congress regime with schemes like seats for women in Panchayati Raj, including those from backward classes.

It's black and white and not hugely sized. But in a prominent position in the paper, it does stand out and make its point. The best part is to have sold them large visual and minimal copy ads. If visuals are worth 1,000 words, as they say, then why drown the consumer with a copy that he will not read. Research has proven that only 3 per cent of consumers read long copy.

I see Tarini getting ready for school. Ma is sitting with her while she has breakfast. My sister is drinking her special tea. She likes it strong. I take the papers across to them and show them the ad. Ma is always supportive. Like all mothers, she looks at it and says '*Bhalo*' in Bengali, which means good. I

कांग्रेस के राज में है हमारी सुनवाई

- पंचायती राज – हमारे हाथ में हमारा राज
- महिलाओं को विशेष अवसर – आज 10 लाख महिला प्रतिनिधि हैं, दलित और आदिवासियों की भी भागीदारी
- अपना विकास अपने हाथ

कांग्रेस–राज्यों में यह प्रगति आज भी जारी है.

Issued by the All India Congress Committee (AICC), 24 Akbar Road, New Delhi-110 001.

कांग्रेस का हाथ
आम आदमी के साथ
www.congress.org.in

Panchayati Raj and work for women. Our voice gets
heard in the Congress regime.

smile at her and tease her. I knew you will say that, I tell her.

Mita, my sister, puts on her specs and reads the copy. She says these facts are good to place before the voter. Tarini also glances at it. She is always observing things quietly.

So, with a little bit of warmth and family time, I am ready to leave for work.

The group of people who are our day-to-day client contacts are mainly Jairam Ramesh, who is the strategy person and Salman Khurshid, the person who looks into strategy translating to creative. They seem like good friends. We figure out they have an IIT-Bombay, MIT and Cambridge education between them. The best minds to work with. Voraji, veteran Congressman and party treasurer, sits in on a lot of general meetings but he is spearheading finance and media negotiations. Ambika Soni and Ahmed Patel are also key members of this team and come in for a lot of meetings.

Of course, make no mistake, Soniaji approves everything at an overall level. Her buy-in is imperative. She does not unnecessarily quibble. And when she makes points, I notice she talks looking at her team. And they, in turn, tell us her requirements. But as I said she is not a fidgeter or iterator for the sake of it. She always surprises us with her in-depth knowledge of India. People, homes, backward classes. And I also find she is particularly sharp on aesthetics. She is very careful about the pictures of Indira Gandhi and Rajiv Gandhi. As also a Dalit lady or an Adivasi person. Whenever she wants to suggest a change, she starts her sentence with 'Can we look at X or Y?' It's never an order.

# CHAPTER 11

## ADD-ONS

ONE OF THE mornings at South Avenue, waiting for the client team to finish some discussions, they are in a huddle. We are at the far end of the main room waiting for some approvals and briefings.

They look towards us and say among themselves, 'Should we ask them?'

We wonder: Now what?

Salman Khurshid asks across the room: 'Will you do our manifesto? Create it? There is very little time. We are planning to be first off the block with the release of the manifesto. Before every other political party. Can you people do it? They want to release it on 22nd March at the AICC headquarters, 24 Akbar Road, at a press conference'.

There seems to be a whiff of changed energy in the air. Body language. A hurry to get up and do things.

The first Phase of the campaign is three quarters through. Feedback is good. Feedback is positive. People are noticing it. Media has picked it up.

*Aam aadmi ko kya mila* is gaining currency.

At the same time, Mrs Gandhi has been on relentless rallies. Many of them each day. Tarun Khiwal is on the rally trail with her, taking the most amazing photographs across the length and breadth of India.

Because she is leading by example, the 118-year-old party

is galvanised into action. Every leader is active, working hard, following suit.

As I said, the winds of change have begun to blow. And as the famous quote goes:

*Sometimes in the wind of change, we find our true direction.*

Has the direction been found? Only time will tell.

Back to the manifesto. Will we do it? Yes, of course. Yes, yes, yes. Two reasons. One is our team is enthusiastic and passionate about the task at hand. Secondly, with so much infrastructure set up for this client back in our office, it would be foolish to let go of work when it's coming to us. And obviously, it's coming to us because trust has been built up between the client and the agency team.

So there begins a briefing on the manifesto! A very important document in any political campaign. It gives out the intent of the party. It is out in the public domain for everyone to see.

A published booklet. The idea is to retrieve the growth and development agenda. To put forth the fact that it is the party that fought for and won India's freedom, ushered in the Green Revolution, created anti-poverty programmes and made India a nuclear space and missile power.

The manifesto that they published in 1999 was unattractive. Boring. This has to be a far better approach. That is the challenge before us.

Rupam asks if he can use colour and not black and white. Here is where he feels it will be important. They are open. Everything is cost-related. No extra money for all the niceties.

Printing in colour always costs more. Prudence shows this is where money will be well spent to bring in optimism and cheer.

Just a few days to create and print it. As usual, very tight deadlines.

All the written matter is taking place within the party. We have to art direct it. Ali, Rupam and Pooja discuss it internally when we reach the agency. They plan to make the cover speak. How? By talking about all the themes:

*Aam aadmi* depiction:

| |
|---|
| Women |
| Soniaji |
| Rajivji |
| Rallies |
| Flags |

A very active and vibrant picture is imperative—which will be an eye-opener and urge the reader to open the manifesto and read it.

Rupam has an idea about how he wants to create it. He speaks to Tarun Khiwal and asks for the transparencies he has been shooting during the rallies with Sonia Gandhi.

Rupam works through the night, going through hundreds of transparencies. Chooses a few and integrates them into a stunning visual. If a viewer looks at it, they may think it's one large picture. It has to tell all the stories of our themes: women, an approachable leader, relentless rallies, common man, happy faces, secularism.

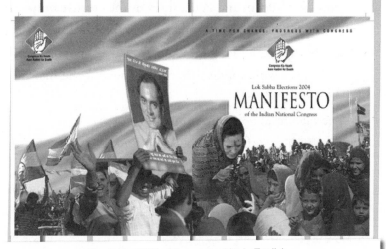

Manifesto 2004 - 28-page booklet in English.

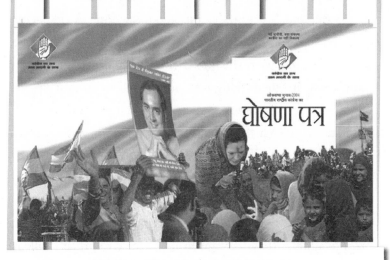

Manifesto 2004 - 28-page booklet in Hindi.

Next day, Rupam and Pooja show us the creative output in English and Hindi. It is breathtaking. No other word. Again, a picture that speaks a thousand words.

Both meet with approval from the client at the first shot. They are all delighted.

The manifesto goes into print.

It's a highly confidential job, with Prantik working on the printing process and the positives.

He is at Express Colour Scan. They have two setups: one in Okhla and the other in Gurgaon. While working at night, he figures the artworks are not in order. Some of the pages are mixed up. Despite so much care and checks and balances, this does happen. But at the last point of scrutiny, it does get caught by Prantik and his team. Thank goodness. Prantik desperately calls up the Associate Creative Director (ACD), who has looked at the client copy on this job. Being their manifesto, the text has come from them. However, he has had to clean it up, and of course, take charge to see there are no language errors at the copy stage. ACD luckily is awake and makes it to the press at Gurugram late at night. The press is in an obscure and lonely place, difficult to find. Somehow, he makes it there. Quickly, he sorts it out.

The Express guys are very good partners. In fact, at the press in Okhla, they have given us a secret room. It's called... any guesses—Khanna 2. All our work for this client gets done there. No other work happens from that room. For any other agency or client.

The manifesto goes into print. Next day, bulk copies get

shipped to the war room at South Avenue. The war room. A few advance copies come to the office. Rupam, Ali and the creative teams are pouring over it. The first impression is that it's very attractive. A solid document. Making a very strident appearance. Once they start leafing through the inside pages suddenly Ali says, 'Wait! What's that?'

The worst nightmare hits us.

There is one page in the centre of the final printed manifesto which is upside down. No, no, no. This can't be happening. Just when they ask us to print a major job. And one so critical. The press conference is a few hours away. Prantik, Vijay and members of Express Colour Scan rush to South Avenue. My instructions are to go through each of the 4,000 copies already delivered there. Check them. Two boys from the press are sent to a local market to buy binders in case we need to remove that page and rebind the copies. What a shoddy job that will be. We are all nervous as hell. Sonia Gandhi and her senior team will be on the dais holding up this book. The press would have a field day once they spot this upside-down page.

As I said, this is a nightmare scenario.

The copies are getting checked at the war room. There is a team of people. The manifestos are spread all over and the faultless ones are piled up in a corner. The process of checking all copies takes three hours because every page of every document is checked. What emerges?

No other copy has that mistake. Usually, in any big job, there is a margin for error. This mistake was in just one copy. And that was the copy that had come to the agency. This is what is loosely called Printer's Devil. In every job, there is a margin of 1 or 2 per cent for that.

What drama. What tension. We felt the rug had been pulled from under our feet. The checked manifestoes, all correct and fine, head for 24 Akbar Road. We are safe for now.

The manifesto reaches in the nick of time.

It is launched with a lot of fanfare at the AICC headquarters. Once the speeches are done, the team on the dais led by the Congress President stands up and holds the manifesto.

People are clamouring for their copies. Everyone is super excited. The media is there in full force. They pick up copies and glance through it. Overall, there is a spirit of a job well done. Powerful speeches. There is also an announcement that on October 2 each year the party will announce the progress of the matters promised in the manifesto.

Party workers across the country are very enthusiastic about receiving the manifesto. They are proud of something at last. After the three drubbings in December, there is positive activity. The last 15 days are a witness to that. This is a colourful solid document giving an intent that ties in with the campaign idea.

We wait for the media reports the next day. However, television channels are already flashing it across everywhere.

'The Congress manifesto takes on issues of unemployment and social inequality. The party assures an inclusive growth, a transparent government, checking central government decisions like divestments taken in the last five years.'

At the agency, we know this is a big victory for the party. At last, they are first off the block for something of significance. If nothing

The backdrop created by Rupam for the Manifesto Launch at AICC headquarters.

THE WEEKLY NEWSMAGAZINE

# OUTLOOK

Rs 15 March 15, 2004

SPECIAL FEATURE
MANAGING YOUR MONEY IN 2004

**EXCLUSIVE NATIONWIDE OPINION POLL**

## NDA SHINES

BJP+allies
# 280-290

CONGRESS+allies
# 159-169

The weekly magazines are meanwhile still publishing cover stories predicting a thumping victory for NDA and allies.

else, it shows intent. Vote us into power and these are our promises.

The biggest point to note is the *Aam aadmi* slogan has come in for loads of discussion. At the press conference, questions are asked. Are you moving away from the *garib* (poverty) platform? '*Garibi hatao!*' has been an erstwhile platform for the party. No, not at all. '*Aam aadmi* includes them' is the response of Sonia Gandhi.

With the manifesto out of the way, we are asked by them if we can design the covers of the Vision documents. Vision documents on defence and economic policy. Long-form texts on these are written and given to us. Covers are designed using the campaign look. Pooja creates a modern contemporary look. It's a big challenge from an art direction point of view. The party is 118 years old. So, to change the logo without changing much is a task in itself. Point to note is that she cleans up the existing hand logo and puts in in a rhombus frame. It looks modern.

We are also asked for a cover design for the chargesheet. In English and Hindi.

All this gets done at breakneck speed. Let me make it clear here: All parties take out all kinds of booklets, posters, stickers and chargesheets. We are learning as we go along. And jobs coming in have to be rendered and returned. That is the essence of political advertising.

Things are moving at whirlwind speed now.

March

Phase 2 of the campaign is on. The Achievements campaign or the Bridge campaign between the Questions Phase and the Future Phase. An advertisement is seen every three days by the target audience and is planned for a period of twelve days. It

# THE
# ECONOMIC GROWTH

### THE CONGRESS AGENDA

The Economic Policy Booklet. Cover design 2004.

# SECURITY, DEFENCE
# AND
# FOREIGN POLICY

### THE CONGRESS AGENDA

Foreign Policy Security and Defence agenda. Cover design 2004.

imparts the right information to the consumer. It tells them in no uncertain terms who created the computer revolution, the green and white and industrial revolutions and many such major developments.

Many rallies are taking place across the country. Political alliances are being discussed every day. Speculation runs high. Marginal and regional parties can make a huge difference.

Given the activity in the Congress party, many regional players are coming forth to pledge support. Mrs Gandhi continues her relentless rallies and briefings across the country amidst the noise of 'foreigner' reverberating through taunts and innuendo.

The agency team has now been at this pace from January 6, two-and-a-half months of intense pressure. The young members are holding up very well. They have put their heart and soul into the job, barely getting sleep and making sure there are no problems along the way.

Dealing with any client is a challenge. Each company comes with its own set of issues.

However, this is NOT just any client.

This is a different deal. Very different. Even if they have been out of power for nine years, they still are the people we have seen rampantly on television and newspapers. They create policies and have run the country. Many of them are respected in their fields. For all of us, this is a new world. Most of all, for our executives who do client-facing work daily, and have to run around for approvals. Go to residences of these people in Lutyens Delhi for translations. Rush to printing presses.

Development and technology. Our voices get heard during the Congress rule.

Green Revolution and schemes for farmers. Our voices get heard during the Congress regime.

On one occasion Kabir and Prantik are at Pranab Mukherjee's house for some approvals. His secretary is also a Mukherjee with a sense of humour! He asks do you want to meet Mukherjee inside or outside?

It's late one night in the last week of March. A call has come from the war room. It sounds urgent.

Change your cellphone numbers, we are told. All of you. The entire team. We have information that your numbers are being tapped. Who? When? How? Nothing more is revealed. Just do it. Straightaway. Gosh. This is now getting scary.

I call in Admin and Finance. Ask them to tighten security and get us new phones. Immediately. It's midnight now. This news has circulated amongst the team. Everyone is a bit anxious. Such messages in the night are scarier.

As I pack up for the day, I see Kabir walking into my room. He has just returned on his bike, on the lonely road leading to the agency ending in the *cul de sac*. He has heard this news as he enters the doors on the third floor.

He sits down. Tears are flowing down his face. I look up, shocked. 'What's happened Kabir?' Kabir is a tall, well-built young man. He tells me: 'I'm sure I will get knocked off on this road'.

I ask Raju, our diligent canteen boy, to get some hot tea. Kabir is just the one person on the team who has expressed emotionally what we are all going through. The challenges of creating so much work so fast, so many new processes, the threat of leaks, the late and long hours. Daily. Everyday. No let up. I realise it's taking a toll on us. Kabir and I drink hot tea.

He calms down. I ask him if he is being followed or has some evidence of what he said. We both realise it's just imagination running wild. Totally natural as you walk in after a hard day late at night and hear that phones are being tapped. How would a 23-year-old react? Soon we are both laughing, and he smiles, assuring me he's feeling better.

Saying goodbye to some people still working, I leave. It's been a very hard day.

# CHAPTER 12

## GAINING MOMENTUM

## MARCH 29

OUR PHONES GET changed first thing in the morning.

The third Phase of the campaign is being shot. This is a large campaign with five half-page print ads in colour. Finally, colour and finally a larger size. Separately for North and South. And three films.

The producer shooting these films in Mumbai is Pankaj Parashar. He has made feature films like *Jalwa* and *Chalbaaz* and also is a veteran ad film maker. He has been a good partner to our Delhi operations on other clients. We zero in on him. Ali has a good rapport with him and briefs him on the working mode on this client. Signs a non-disclosure agreement and gets a competitive quote. He has quoted the lowest amongst the three mandatory offers.

Print photography is a large job. Let me explain why. Each subject will be shot twice. One with a North Indian face and the other with a South Indian face. This newspaper campaign has five ads with the same target audience. In any campaign, you have to stick to the defined target you have set at the beginning.

Why two faces of each ad? Because it's all about relatability. India is such a vast country. In every state or zone, people look distinct and talk different languages and dialects. The state of Kerala is very distinct from UP. And so on and so forth. If you release an ad in Karnataka with a face from Bengal, it does not resonate. Relatability reduces. So Rupam had the challenge of shooting ten ads.

Ali, Rupam and team are in Mumbai for the film shoot. Pankaj has set it up very carefully. These films are positive and futuristic in their narrative.

They will depict a farmer who is happily awaiting the return of the Congress party. Which will bring back happy days.

Women who ask for their rights and their voices get heard.

And youth who are employed again.

This campaign is '*Is liye main Congress ke saath hoon*'. (This is why I am with the Congress.)

Once again, there is very little copy. Just the six basics of governance. They promise these pillars if they are voted back to power.

| |
|---|
| Gramin Vikas (Rural Development) |
| Yuva Rozgar (Employment for youth) |
| Mahila Sahastikaran (Women's empowerment) |
| Samajik Sadhbhavna (Social harmony) |
| Saman Avsar (Equal opportunity) |
| Aarthik Navothan (Economic renewal) |

Other major facts they want to drive home are equality and secularism. Also, growth across India.

## APRIL 3

Television news announcements start. Remember I told you we had the news playing in my room, the client management department, and the creative area. Our Associate Creative Director, who is into politics, comes across to my room. He says, 'Are you watching the news?' Actually, not right now.

The Election Commission (EC) has announced a lifting of the ban on political advertising on television. The Indian Broadcasters Federation (IBF) has been in dialogue with them. That's news. Big news. Now each party will be busy making films and the channels will get a lot of airtime from the competing parties. There is one caveat, though. The films will have to be shown to the offices of the EC and prior approval will have to be sought before they can go on air. Any film not meeting their criteria will not be approved for telecast.

Our films are currently being shot in Mumbai. Great timing. This development gets conveyed immediately to the team there. Our scripts are positive and have no nasty salvos. However, we are doubly careful not to violate any norm. Axed films would mean reshooting and there's hardly any time before the first Phase of polling starts on April 20. The ads will go off the air by May 19 as per polling guidelines. Therefore just 15 days to see the campaign by the target audience.

The print campaign with its dual faces for North and South is almost ready. Translations are going via the secret process to the Mumbai office. Approvals are happening with the powers-that-be in the Congress party.

Pankaj Parashar comes down to Delhi with the finished films. He arrives at our office and observes the frenzy. Rupam and team have finalised all the print ads. The final films are with Pankaj. We assemble in the conference room to see the films.

There are three films. Again, all keeping with our target groups and responding to the questions raised in the first Phase.

The story lines of the 30-second films are outlined below.

- A set of three unemployed youth, sitting together and talking. In the backdrop, there is a closed factory. It looks like a small town. They are happy, discussing that jobs will be back once the Congress comes back to power.

- A woman in a public transport bus asks a man to get up from her reserved seat. Raises her voice. Says we women will be heard once the Congress comes to power.

- A happy farmer walking with his son in a field. Telling him better days will come for him and they won't go hungry once the Congress comes to power.

The films for television are simple, clear and communicate the point unambiguously. They are in colour, unlike the Phase 1 films which were stark black and white. This is the Vision Phase which projects a positive outlook. Therefore, the use of colour.

We all leave for South Avenue, Pankaj Included. As usual, deadlines are tight and the ads literally have to start appearing next morning for states going to polls on April 20. At least 10-15 days of telecast would be required for consumers to retain the main messages of the campaign.

The war room is crowded, a far cry from when we went there for the first time. When silence prevailed and it was sparsely populated. Today, there is no place to sit or move. The elections are around the corner and positive energy has suffused the party. People are visiting, dropping by, and discussing. Often, we see celebrities and corporate business heads who are joining the party at this stage.

On seeing us, they clear out the front room and tell us to set up quickly. The large screen television is set up as is the sound system. Pankaj is looking around this interesting yet alien scene. A filmmaker from Mumbai in a political hub. Would be interesting to get his take once we exit. Unlike the practice of taking the finished campaign to 10 Janpath, for this Phase the work has directly come here. Mrs Gandhi is on rallies outside Delhi. Since approvals are urgently required, she will see it as she returns.

We show the print campaign first. Five half-page colour advertisements.

- Women and how jobs will get created as they were in the past.
- Unemployed youth who will have more jobs to look forward to.
- Petty investors whose money will be secure.
- Farmers who will have friendly schemes.
- Technology and progress as in past Congress regimes.

"कांग्रेस ही कम्प्यूटर क्रान्ति ले कर आई, और आगे चली टेक्नोलॉजी में लीडर भी बनाएगी। इसलिए

# मैं कांग्रेस के साथ हूँ।"

"The Congress ushered in the computer revolution, and will also make us a worldbeater in technology. Isliye

## main Congress ke saath hoon."

The Congress Party's far-sighted policies brought computers to India, started the PCO revolution, and took TV to the masses. The Congress will take the country even further, on the path of progress, in the years to come.

Six Basics of Governance:
• Samajik Sadbhavna.
• Yuva Rozgar.
• Grameen Vikas.
• Arthik Navotthan.
• Mahila Sashaktikaran.
• Saman Avsar.

Congress Ka Haath
Aam Aadmi Ke Saath
www.congress.org.in

Same ad for North and South zones—employment for women.

# मैं कांग्रेस के साथ हूँ."

रोजगार और विकास

कांग्रेस का इरादा है रोजगार देने का कि एक युवक के लिए नौकरी से बढ़ कर खुशी कुछ नहीं हो सकती है. तभी तो, कांग्रेस शासन में लोगों के लिए रोजगार के अनगिनत अवसर पैदा किए.

कांग्रेस के मूल सिद्धांत:

- सामाजिक सद्भावना और सुरक्षा
- हर व्यक्ति को एक रोजगार
- किसानों एवं खेत मजदूरों का सम्पन्न भविष्य
- महिलाओं का सशक्तिकरण
- आर्थिक नवोत्थान
- कमजोर व पिछड़े वर्ग की भागीदारी

कांग्रेस का साथ
आम आदमी के साथ
www.congress.org.in

---

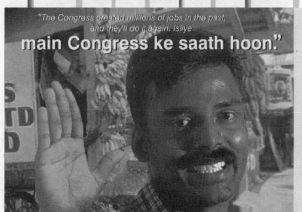

"The Congress created millions of jobs in the past,
and they'll do it again. Isliye

# main Congress ke saath hoon."

Growth
with
Harmony

Before anything else, what a young person needs is a job. Which is why it was always a Congress priority to generate employment opportunities.

Six Basics of Governance:

- Samajik Sadbhavna.
- Yuva Rozgar.
- Grameen Vikas.
- Arthik Navotthan.
- Mahila Sashaktikaran.
- Saman Avsar.

Congress Ka Hauth
Aam Aadmi Ke Saath
www.congress.org.in

Employment for youth.

Better days for farmers when the Congress returns to power.

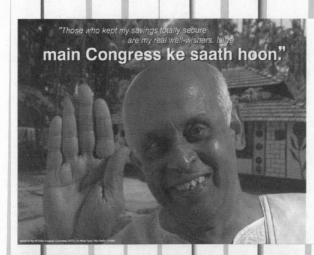

Safety for middle class investors.

Employment for women in the Panchayati Raj.

Key phrase in this Vision campaign: *Sadbhavna aur vikas* (Harmony with growth). These themes are part of rally speeches and all written material. Differentiators for the party in their campaign image as the national party that delivers growth and protects secularism.

It's been almost three months of working with this client. There is huge learning on our side of the issues, requirements, the kind of slant and direction they desire. The campaign is based on what we had presented at our pitch. There has been a lot of strategic contribution from Jairam Ramesh and Salman Khurshid. It's been tweaked and polished and finished with real photography and not representative stock pictures. Of course, the six basics of governance have been added now and the ads are getting presented in Hindi first, followed by English. Once they are approved, they will get translated into regional languages and go to each state for release.

The ads get approved without major changes. Just a couple of minor glitches but nothing of significance. No change of models or pictures or copy.

That's a relief. The servicing team is already planning to go back and execute the ads for release. Lots of overnight work ahead for the studio and media teams as well.

Salman Khurshid signs off the ads except for a couple which will be changed and brought back.

Now the films are presented. The television screen comes to life and the films play out. They get seen twice by Khurshid, Jairam Ramesh, Motilal Vora, Ambika Soni and Ahmed Patel. They approve the films without a single change. Not one.

It's all ok. A few of the others working out of South Avenue including Shamim and some young executives are shown the films. They like them. They are working to the brief. There's a lot of excitement.

Pankaj was definitely expecting changes. He is meeting a political group like this perhaps for the first time. He is totally surprised that it took them literally 15 minutes to approve the films. He is taking the night flight back to Mumbai. All the languages will be dubbed, and the regional films will have to be finished. He will hurry the job out in a day, he promises. All under strict security.

Meanwhile, the EC has asked to see the finished films of all parties for approval. Nothing without their stamp will be accepted by any television channel. From our side, Ali and the client-side Jairam Ramesh go to the offices of the EC. A lot of parties are in line to show their material. By that, I mean finished films. Our films are the only ones that get approved on that day without a change. All the others are marked with changes. Which means they will have a delay and we will be the first to get off the block. Our films are straight and honest and are only talking about a future vision.

I'm thinking to myself as I reach the office how smoothly Phase 3, the longest phase of the campaign, went. We, as a team, have learnt exponentially. They as a team have learnt to trust us and the process much more. Two phases of the campaign have run in mass media. The *Aam aadmi ko kya mila* and the Achievements campaigns—both have worked well. Very well so far. Feedback has been good. We are at a midway point of the campaign effort. Despite a much smaller budget, sharp thinking and an insightful creative process have led to denting the narrative of the competitor thus far.

As I sit back and chat with Prince in my office, I tell him to prepare for an onslaught of cheque making. Reams of press and television releases are due over the next month. He jokes with me: 'Well, we will make the cheques, but you will sign them. So be prepared to sign at all odd hours'. I have signed 300-400 cheques on a heavy day.

I ask him how his relationship with the finance department at AICC is holding up. He says it's very professional. He gives them advance notice for the cheque as we have to pay advance to media. Cheques are always ready on time. He has built a good rapport with Voraji and his assistants. No delays. And whatever is promised to clear release orders is given in full.

Prince leaves my room.

I just think of all the myths I have known or believed so far.

1.  Politicians will keep you waiting forever. The point is they are on time for all meetings. Every time. It's we who are always almost late. Not very, 10 minutes for sure.

    I wonder what it is with our industry—why can't we show up on time. Mostly it's work just happening at the last minute. Paste-ups of layouts or printouts being grabbed. Taking chances and living on the edge.

2.  They will all be 'Not like us'. Strangely, we find some of them pretty cool.

3.  The team we deal with day to day are highly qualified:

IIT, Cambridge, MIT, Jamia, etc.

4. Payments will be dicey and shady. Surprisingly not.

5. We will wait in corridors for hours—for meetings, approvals. Has not happened so far. In fact, they are infuriatingly and irritatingly on time.

Let's see if this holds up till the end of the elections.

# CHAPTER 13

## CRISIS

POOJA COMES INTO my room. She looks so tired. Days on end of working late hours and keeping her eyes on the screen. Checking and rechecking layouts and artworks. Not easy. She is keen to know what's happened at the meeting. I tell her how it was so easy this time. Hardly any changes.

The first Phase was so much harder. Changing films and print ads. I told her to brace herself for an avalanche of work. She tells me a funny anecdote. The lease on her house is expiring soon. She has been house-hunting on Sunday with her husband. A broker is showing them options. They take a break for lunch. They invite the broker to join them. Halfway through, the broker and her husband realise she's very quiet. Only to see she's fast asleep! After a while, she whispers to her husband: 'Let's skip the rest of this house hunting trip. Please let's pay the escalation the landlord is demanding. And carry on at our current address. I'm tired and I can't shift homes in the middle of this workload!' I'm smiling at her anecdote when we are brought back to the present.

Some loud conversations are taking place outside Ali's room. Both Pooja and I turn to see what's happened. One of the young executives is in tears. What's the drama that's happening? What is this crisis now? It's late evening and all of us have had a long day.

Now here is what the young lady executive is saying. She

has purchased an image for the urban campaign from a private source. Not a public image bank, where anyway we had decided not to go for purposes of confidentiality. So, she has used a small private collection of a young girl living in Lutyens Delhi and bought an image for a fee. Everything has been paid for.

'So, what's the problem?' Ali is asking her.

I'm standing on the side watching. Why is she white as a sheet and nervous, with eyes misting?

She had forgotten to add in the contract that she is buying this image for a political campaign. She had called her an hour ago to say she is sending an addendum to the Letter of Agreement that this is for political advertising and this person concerned should sign saying she has no objection! We were just being extra cautious as people get a bit sticky with political alignments and messages. Some like this Lutyens Delhi lady clearly did not want any involvement.

And, unfortunately, the image owner was in that category of people. She did not want any involvement!

She was furious: 'You've duped me.'

So, Ali tells the young executive in tears not to worry. He knows for sure this has not been done on purpose. What would be in our interest is not to publish this picture and return it to the angry lady. This is a genuine mistake. In the tsunami of work, this minor detail which now seems major has been missed out.

Now on further investigation, it is found that the colour positives have been made and sent to *India Today* already. Prantik looks at his records and confirms this. Someone is saying tell media department to talk to *India Today*. Someone is rushing into the Starcom office next door telling them to pull out that ad. 'Tell them to cancel. Tell them to return it. Tell them we will replace it in a couple of days.'

Starcom quickly calls up *India Today* to find the status of this ad. Mistakes happen all the time. As long as agencies and clients have existed, mistakes have happened. Starcom gets the urgency and tension.

Now unfolds another nightmare. *India Today* confirms that the issue is in print. Right now. On the machines. Copy upon copy is getting printed as we speak.

This is a crisis with ramifications. The furious lady has threatened to send a legal notice. So now we are done. Cooked. Baked. Spat out.

My mind races. For all the hiding, concealing and confidentiality of the mission, for all the checks and balances, for all the rules and regulations, a small oversight like this is going to result in shame. The media will have a field day. The client will be called names. Our agency will be hauled over the coals. Everything looks like it's ending. All eyes are on me now. Ali, Prantik the young executive and the small crowd that has gathered. What do we do?

What can we do? Nothing except apologise. That has happened. I decide very fast. I need to inform my boss and the client. It's best they know in advance.

I go to my room. It's about 7 pm. Getting dark in more ways than one. Shut the lights. Keep my back to the door and sit in a corner where no one can see me. If I am going to get yelled at, I don't want anyone in my office to witness it. Basically, I am hiding.

I first call Arvind, my boss and CEO of the agency. He picks up quickly. He has now understood that if there's a call from me, it's urgent. I don't have time for casual calls given the workload of the last few months.

His reaction? He hears me out. 'Shit happens', he says. 'We will deal with the consequences. Don't worry about a thing.' This time he ends—'You have my 2,000 per cent support.'

I guess far away in Mumbai, he is calmer than any of us. Arvind is an optimist. Nothing really fazes him.

Next, I call Jairam Ramesh. As usual, he is in a rush. 'Ok, tell me quickly in two minutes.'

I say, 'Two minutes will not work. I need ten.'

He calls back in a bit. I am still in my room. I explain what's happened. His first reaction. 'How many atom bombs are you guys going to throw on me?' he explodes.

'Well, really this is the first one,' I confess. And I hope the last. He then proceeds to say he will sort it out as he knows the person concerned.

I say, 'You'll make it worse. She doesn't want any dealing on this topic. This is a call to inform you'.

He gets it. Says, 'Let's wait and watch'.

Now I walk out of my room, both calls done. All worried eyes are on me. I tell them I have spoken and, fortunately, no one reacted adversely. I had to keep things calm outside.

We decide to wait for the legal notice. And deal with it head-on. What option do we have? Sigh.

Ali says, 'Come and have tea in my room.' We wonder how this happened. In the larger scheme of things, we wonder why such a slip took place despite so many checks and balances and careful planning.

If there is a time we are really scared, it's this.

The agency is buzzing with life as Phase 3—the Vision Phase of the campaign is into full throttle production.

I can't help anyone tonight. They all know their job and are competent, notwithstanding the error on the contract for that one picture. Music is playing loud, the news is blaring somewhere, food is being ordered, laughter sounds are emanating from a distance, and lights are shining brightly all over the agency. I stand outside my room and turn around to see my room. Suddenly quiet.

Another crazy day ends for me but not for my team. In the car, as usual, it's dark and late. My head is heavy with tension, thinking about the legal notice. I make the journey back quietly. No music tonight.

# CHAPTER 14

## 'HURRY, HURRY'

I GET A call. It's the client. They want an urgent meeting. Goodness, are they rethinking their approvals of the previous day? Let it not be. I am now ready to scream if there are changes.

With trepidation, using my most business-like voice I say. 'Sure. Why?'

'We want to brief you on something. You will have to show it very fast. Latest tomorrow.' Oh, new work? Great. As an office head, I see growth in each new and additional piece of work we get. I also feel happy they are trusting us with more and more work.

'Ok, so what time?'

'10 am. 10 Janpath.'

'Oh.'

*What is this work?*

I immediately call Ali and Rupam and tell them to meet me at 9.45 am at 10 Janpath. Somehow, they always pick up in the first three rings. We all do. The entire team. Looks like we sleep very late and wake up very early. Everyone is always available. 'Let's not be late,' I say. And since we don't know what this is, I decide to keep the team small. Just let the three of us attend this one. Anyway, the rest of the team is busy executing Phase 3 of the campaign.

It's getting hot in Delhi. Temperatures are inching closer to 40. I wear a light-coloured outfit, a far cry from my favourite blacks all through winter.

On reaching, I go inside the security area to make my gate pass. Ali and Rupam have not reached. It's 9.50 am.

I am texting them on those confidential phones.

'Where the **** are you guys?' I press the send button and look up. I see them both walking towards me. Smiling. 'You must be texting us, right?' they tease. I affirm rather sheepishly. What is it with advertising people? We almost don't make it anywhere and then miraculously we do. In the nick of time. Every time.

We have been in and out of these premises so many times now that it's all less daunting. After clearing security, heading towards the office area, I notice the green manicured lawns and the tall hedges. Pretty.

We still don't know what we are meeting for. Wait for a couple of minutes outside the main meeting room. This is a small room with chairs. Large windows with fern plants covering the inside from outside views. Fans are whirring. Flashback to the first time we came here. So cold. So terrifying. Winter gave way to spring and summer is soon setting in. It's just been three months but feels like three years.

We are asked to go inside. Priyanka and Rahul are seated. Cordialities are exchanged. There is an unknown gentleman sitting with them on that oval table, someone we are seeing for the first time. He is a family friend and an erstwhile advertising professional who has been involved with Rajiv Gandhi in his previous campaigns. He wants to review all the material. Our hearts sink. Hope he doesn't make drastic changes, is our collective wish. He quickly goes through the campaigns. Makes a couple of comments. Nothing major. Phew!

Actually, we are being briefed on new jobs. Now that the campaign has gained momentum, there is a desperate need for collateral material. Currently, all the workers in the different states are very enthusiastic, producing their own stickers and posters to underpin the mass media campaign. Now they want to centrally decide the posters and stickers and ship them across the entire nation. This is fantastic. We are all in sync. This is a true campaign. Where every piece of communication reinforces the single-minded theme. Where the thought is contextual and powerful. And not individual random pieces of work.

So, we are asked to do posters and stickers and radio spots. Radio is still banned but we decide to produce the spots. Just like television. If the ban is lifted, we should be the first off the block. And at the village level there are enormous uses for radio spots.

All this needs to be shown by tomorrow. In political campaigns, the role of the poster, sticker, banner, streamer, flag, rally backdrop and small badge is critical. Especially with this campaign being regional, for the common man. The person who is in the bazaars, small shops, markets, street corners. The people who sit under trees by the village well, cycle miles to work, look at wall paintings and hear the radio in the fields or in his shop. Women who have the radio as a companion while cooking and doing housework. It's a direct message to them.

Not a secondary or reminder medium as it's often called.

A primary medium in many ways for political campaigns. Another difference I note in the world of political brands.

A briefing-cum-brainstorming session is in progress. Today we haven't been offered coffee. How to ask? How can you use your brains without caffeine? It's noon. I decide to 'lose all shame' and ask, 'Is it possible to have some tea or coffee?' All the time wishing it is that wonderful aromatic delicious coffee special to this place. Rahul and Priyanka both say 'Of course' and wonder how they forgot to ask.

This meeting carries on for an hour.

Eight poster themes are debated and decided upon.

Secularism

Sacrifice

Growth and harmony

Equality of women

Three poster themes of the Congress President.

Stickers should be easy to read and to the point.

Radio themes are decided. They are to follow the campaign. More like an amalgamation of phases 1 and 2.

We have to present all the work the next day. All to be translated in multiple Indian languages, printed centrally from Delhi and disseminated across the country. To be up in a maximum 5-7 days. Not a minute to lose.

Rupam is centrestage on this one. Especially the posters to be shot for Mrs Gandhi.

This is a huge challenge because she is on a hectic travel plan across the country. Rally upon rally, helicopter rides, traipsing all over the place. Deep into districts, towns and villages. Integrating the same points and messages that the campaign has also put forth among other messages in her speech.

From all sides, things are getting reinforced. Speeches. Websites. Communications. Below the line activations.

Now back to the task ahead. Rupam chooses Tarun Khiwal to do this shoot. Tarun and he have worked together and have a good rapport. Tarun is an award-winning photographer who has made his mark in many areas, one of them being fashion. This shoot is not going to be a boring 'two minute-hurry-hurry-let's gets a picture' affair. Rupam wants portraits. He wants to project her as the lady we have been meeting and getting to know well. Hard-working, polite, and an approachable leader. Also, young enough. At 57 years old, she is young compared to veteran politicians. AB Vajpayee is 80 years at the moment.

Tarun comes on board.

Time is sought with her. A small window of opportunity emerges the next day. Rupam and Tarun go to 10 Janpath. There's a long wait. She's busy in meetings. There is no stylist, make-up artist or coordinator at the shoot. Finally, she makes it. They have set up the camera. Ambika Soni and Priyanka Vadra are also present. Soniaji walks in and tells them upfront 'I am a difficult subject to shoot' with a slight smile on her face.

Her domestic help brings in a variety of sarees. Tarun and Rupam make some choices. She is quick to change and give shots. Light day-time makeup. Nothing extra. Very cooperative. They shoot a lot. But somehow Rupam is not satisfied. He knows he's not got his shots. The ones he has planned. Someone smiling. Thoughtful. The shots are formal. Straightforward. When Soniaji goes in for a saree changeover, he expresses his objective to Ambika Soni and Priyanka. They get it. They say now we have to get her to smile.

As she returns, they start discussing a famous politician who is funny. Narrate anecdotes. This does the trick. There are smiles all around. Tarun is clicking away. Rupam has got his shots, he believes.

Rupam returns to the office. We are all waiting to hear details. He tells us, post the shoot, Priyanka and Tarun and he got talking about photography. She showed them Rajiv Gandhi's collections in their library room. They were to be exhibited overseas soon. He was a keen photographer. She gifted them both a book of his photographs. Wrote a nice message inside. He shows it to us.

He tells us an interesting snippet from his day.

While the book is getting signed by Priyanka, Mrs Gandhi leaves for another large meeting about to happen in the next room. All the senior party leaders are waiting. Tarun and Rupam have been offered coffee and they are sitting in a corner gulping it fast, though it's scalding hot. All the gentlemen are milling around having conversations. Rupam nods to Tarun, let's leave. Mrs. Gandhi has returned by now and spots them gathering their material and cameras. She comes up to them and says have your coffee in peace. Then you can leave. Not before that.

Nice ending to a challenging event.

Meanwhile, in the agency, in a corner of the creative department, Pooja and Sanjiv are busy creating posters. Some transparencies have come from the party. The ones of Indira Gandhi and Rajiv Gandhi. They are old and not of the best quality. The rest we need to shoot. The task is to find real people of all religions to depict secularism. Muslim, Sikh, Jain, Buddhist, Christian, Hindu, etc.

Sanjiv writes two types of sticker campaigns. One aggressive set of messages highlighting the loopholes of the competitor, the other being the promises of what will happen if Congress comes to power. Future intentions.

It's not as if the Congress is the only party making these types of stickers and posters. All of them are indulging in hitting out at competitors. As the polling dates are getting closer, it's Brand Wars out there.

Now a lot of this work is for the three-second medium. Why do I say that? Because research has proven that outdoor advertising in a city is a fleeting medium. At best a reminder. And timing wise it is thought that the consumer will be able to see it for approximately three seconds. However, in villages and small towns where people walk a lot, or cycle to work, they definitely have more time to absorb the message. Again, another differentiator for political brands.

Radio spots are ready. Sanjiv and Kosty have worked on them. Given below is one example of the scripts being developed.

*Aaj mere dost ka janmadin hai. Pachchis saal tak hum dono*

*saath padhe, saath bade hue, hamara dharm kabhi hamare beech mein nahin aaya.*

(Today is my friend's birthday. For 25 years, we studied together, grew up together. Our religion never came between us.)

*Pichhle kuch dino se kai buri khabrein aa rahi hain. Dangon ki, ladaaiyon ki.*

(The past few days have brought news of riots, fights.)

*Kal woh mujhe bazaar mein dikha tha. Us ne muh pher liya.*

(Yesterday I saw him in the market. He turned his head away.)

*Hamare beech jo daraar paida ho gayi hai usey toh main shayad nahin badal sakta.*

(I cannot break the wall that has come up between us.)

*Lekin is baar mujhe kuchh badalna hai.*

(But this time I will change things.)

*Is baar main haalaat badalne wala hoon.*

(This time I will change the circumstances.)

The campaigns for collaterals are ready.

Eight posters

Around twenty designs for stickers.

Standees.

Banners, large and small.

There is a meeting to present these in the war room the next afternoon.

January's silent little ground floor flat is buzzing with life in April. It's packed with people and bursting at the seams.

The front room is cleared out as usual when we present work. Confidentiality is still very much the name of the game.

This time, apart from the usual team of Jairam Ramesh, Salman Khurshid, Ambika Soni and Motilal Vora, there are a few more Congressmen. They have not been present in any significant way before. Like Janardhan Dwivedi, rumoured to be Madam's Hindi speechwriter. He adds the word '*Sochiye*' in the posters that follow. A strong input. As you must have figured, the process has been pretty collaborative so far.

Sanjiv, Rupam and Ali are presenting the big layouts with the creatives.

The vision for this century. Every Indian is the same. Think! Vote for Congress.

Why are they afraid of a woman? Think! Vote for Congress.

वे सिर्फ़ अपना विकास चाहते हैं,
हम भाईचारा और सबका विकास चाहते हैं।

सोचिए!
कांग्रेस को वोट दीजिए

कांग्रेस का हाथ
आम नागरिक के साथ

They only want their development. We want progress for all. Think! Vote for
Congress.

उनके काम
और बलिदान
हमारी दिशा,
देश का मान

सोचिए!
कांग्रेस को वोट दीजिए

कांग्रेस का हाथ
आम आदमी के साथ

Their efforts and sacrifices gave us direction and raised respect for our country.
Think! Vote for Congress.

# कांग्रेस का संकल्प

## किसानों की ख़ुशहाली
## महिलाओं को हक़
## नौजवानों को शिक्षा और रोज़गार

## सबके साथ न्याय

## सोचिए!
### कांग्रेस को वोट दीजिए

### हाथ आपका
### साथ आपका

Congress resolves: Farmers' well-being. Women's rights. Education and employment for youth. Justice for all. Think! Vote for Congress.

One of the gentlemen from their end, not someone we met often, decides to change each and every line, and also the baseline. The slogan!

So now begins the whole process of explaining that you cannot have print and TV saying something and the below-the-line material saying something else. The consumer will get confused.

His suggestions are Congress *ka haath jan jan ke saath* and so on and so forth. For each poster, he is suggesting a new baseline. That's eight baselines!

Against every rule of good communication.

It takes a long time to make him understand. He is not convinced. Anyway, we have to do the right thing. To give in, we accept many of his headline changes. But the slogan remains intact.

In the life and times of an agency, these are the challenges you encounter. Again, another difference with 'normal' clients. There is one marketing head.

Next, the stickers are presented.

Must report that the three posters with Sonia Gandhi's portraits have been met with a gasp of surprise. They achieve what is desired. Approachable. Younger than the powers-that-be in the opposite party.

And very arresting. The client team is very happy with these.

सबको खुशहाल बनाना है
तो कांग्रेस को वापस लाना है

कांग्रेस का हाथ
आम आदमी के साथ

पेट भर खाना है
तो कांग्रेस को वापस लाना है

कांग्रेस का हाथ
आम आदमी के साथ

भेद–भाव भगाना है
तो कांग्रेस को वापस लाना है

कांग्रेस का हाथ
आम आदमी के साथ

घोटालों से छुटकारा पाना है
तो कांग्रेस को वापस लाना है

कांग्रेस का हाथ
आम आदमी के साथ

बेरोज़गारी भगाना है
तो कांग्रेस को वापस लाना है

कांग्रेस का हाथ
आम आदमी के साथ

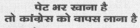

The Sticker Campaign.

"मेरा सपना, समृद्ध और प्रगतिशील भारत अपना."

कांग्रेस का हाथ
आम आदमी के साथ

My dream—A prosperous and progressive India.

Road show, rally and meeting backdrops. Loads of pictures shot of Soniaji at work depicting the hectic travels, dynamism, activity, energy, approachability and friendliness of the lady. All combined by Rupam to create a picture that talks.

"भेद-भाव मिटाना है,
देश समृद्ध बनाना है."

कांग्रेस का हाथ
आम आदमी के साथ

We have to remove discrimination and make the country prosper.

# आइए, बनाएं देश महान
# करें राष्ट्र का नव निर्माण

निर्माण

कांग्रेस का हाथ
आम आदमी के साथ

Come let's build the country anew and create a great India.

It's late. The creative team leaves. They have to make the changes and get into artworks. Complete the signing process, including bringing back the entire lot to Salman Khurshid, for final approval. Prantik will then get the print production progressives done and hand them over to Shamim. All printing is going to be centralised and disseminated from Delhi across the country. It's a humongous task. This is a general election! One that comes only once in five years and is dealing with the biggest target audience in the world.

All to be done in the next two days.

Ali and I stay back. Anita joins us. It's about 7 pm. *India Today* has suggested an Impact feature to Jairam Ramesh and team. He wants to discuss this urgently.

'Should we or should we not' is the question he is asking.

The proposal is that they will run three features over consecutive weeks in their English, Hindi and Telugu magazines. These are special features which will be printed on art paper and provided by us. They will staple it into the magazine prominently.

The bustle and drama of the election phases are on us. All actions to start from 20th of this month. It's a good idea to be seen and heard as much as possible now. Or as they say, to peak at the right time.

Now, this is making sense. Andhra Pradesh is a strong territory for the Congress. Reddy has been very active there. We have seen him at the war room several times. English communication is a good idea for urban fence-sitters and loyalists. And covering the Hindi belt is also required. For the same reasons.

All of us feel it's worth doing it. Anita says she will ensure the best rates and prominent positions in the magazine. She will also help to negotiate dates of release. We want to time them close to the polling phases. All that has to be looked into and scheduling has to be done accordingly.

The issue is its three blank pieces of art paper. All to be created from scratch. Written, art directed, photographed and printed.

We get into a brainstorming session. What can these themes be? We are now in April and the elections are literally on us. The political temperature in the country is high. Every party is shouting their messages out loud.

More cups of tea come from the canteen. Ramesh, Anita, Ali and I are in discussions. Ramesh is clear-headed, razor sharp and it's always a challenge to work with him.

Three themes are decided:

1. Productivity and growth of the agrarian economy from Independence.
2. Building up of modern India. Industry, PSU, education institutions and technology.
3. The Congress charter. What will they stand for if they come to power? Themes of secularism, inclusiveness and togetherness to build the country and go ahead.

Lots of work looming up, lots to do. As always this is required 'yesterday', to use an irritating cliche.

Before making the long drive back we need a comfort break. What are the difficulties of being a woman in the workplace?

This is a major one. This place has only one toilet, used by all and sundry. Let me not get graphic. I have often excused myself and made a quick dash to a nearby hotel to use their facilities. Today, I am stuck.

I ask the helper boy to check if it is clean. He knows me by now. He goes in and returns after five minutes. Now you can go, he says.

On the drive back, I observe Ali is very quiet. Not his usual self-making wisecracks, funny observations about the meeting gone by. In fact, I have noticed this over the last few days.

I ask him hesitantly if everything is ok. He replies after a few seconds.

'I'm deciding where I will expend my energy. I'm just too tired. So am saving it for what is really required,' he says. 'After all, it's the same quota of energy. I have to decide where to spend it.'

*Hmmm. Wise, I note. Life's lessons in small nuggets.*

We are all quiet for the rest of the journey. Lost in thought. So much has happened these last few months. So many types of new people, new experiences and new surprises. Like the Impact feature.

As the 118-year-old party comes to life, there is movement and energy in the form of rallies, coalitions, meetings, advertisements, manifestos, vision documents, chargesheets, across the length and breadth of the country—the impetus for additional spend should be hopefully more open. The Impact feature, below-the-line activities are not budgeted in the initial amount. Additional budgets will have to be sanctioned.

Our Associate Creative Director will do the Impact features. He is politically inclined and knows the issues well. Ali briefs him on the discussions at the meeting. He has a lot of writing to do. Long copy. We are lucky—he is the best man for the job. Hopefully being a magazine feature, people will read the details. Unlike newspapers, which perish as a daily product, a weekly lies around in the house or office for seven days. Research has proved that a magazine gets picked up several times to get read.

Pooja is the art director. By now she's familiar with all the multiple shoots and transparencies we have. She will have to see how much she can use from our stock and how much new photography she would need to do. She calls up Pankaj, the photographer, we have been using, and lines him up for the photography requirements. He has been a good partner to the creative effort. Adding a lot and being available to meet urgent requirements.

They get to work. It's midnight.

## APRIL 8

The Impact features are ready. Three features of three pages each. All factual and true.

The copy meets with instant approval, barring a few minor changes. Since it's written in English for a change, the Hindi and Telegu translations need to be done urgently.

However, what goes into a major tailspin are the pictures of the past leaders. Jawaharlal Nehru, Indira Gandhi, Rajiv Gandhi, Lal Bahadur Shastri and PV Narasimha Rao. They don't like the pictures we've used. And we have used the best we have. Archives are barren at their end. The difficulty being that we cannot procure pictures from publications due to the secret nature of the work we are doing.

We are asked to check in a Khan Market studio where the family has taken photographs over the years.

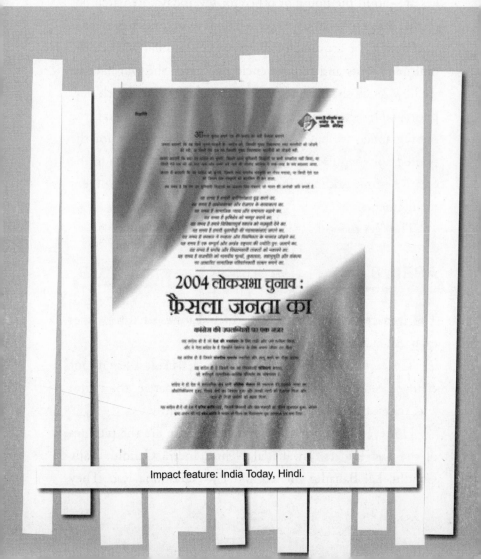

Impact feature: India Today, Hindi.

Impact feature: Building India. The Agrarian Economy.

Impact feature: Building of Industry.

Impact feature: India Today.

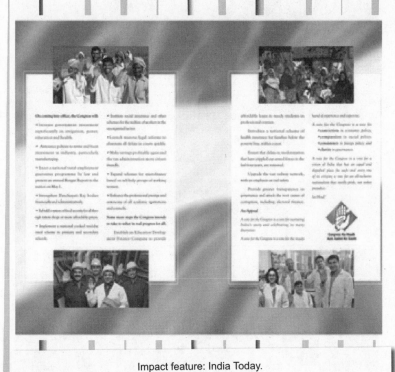

Impact feature: India Today.

Finally, after a lot of ups and downs, the appropriate pictures are found and approved.

The printing of these features, since they are not regular ads, have to be done by us. Prantik and team, already overloaded with posters and stickers, take on this task too. His partners at Express Colour Scan and Thompson Press have been exemplary in support. If our office was working nights, so were they.

Let me remind you that the polls are going to take place on the following dates.

| | |
|---|---|
| 20th April: | 141 constituencies, 16 states and union territories. |
| 26th April: | 137 constituencies, 11 states and union territories. |
| 5th May: | 83 constituencies, 7 states and union territories. |
| 10th May: | 182 constituencies, 16 states and union territories. |

# CHAPTER 15

## AMBUSH TIME

ANOTHER MAJOR CAMPAIGN which is quietly taking shape is what we call the Ambush campaign. It also has other names in the agency. Urban campaign. Kosty is the creator and architect of this creative approach. He has written it so powerfully and been so passionate about it that he literally did the first cut of art direction on it. Of course, Pooja and Rupam did take care of his vision from a formal art point of view and photography. Kosty attended a few shoots on this campaign too. It has the same themes as the overall campaign. The *Aam aadmi's* travails.

The unemployed youth ad has run already in *India Today, Outlook, The Week, Femina, Women's Era*. Followed by the one on the middle-class investor losing savings.

This campaign has started in the second-half of March and comes once every week. It has a totally different look and feel. Since it is for urban India, it is stylish and classy. One-line hard-hitting copy and the '*Aam aadmi*' slogan.

The creatives want a colour ad, but it gives a black and white feel. This is four-colour black and white printing, a newish method of printing in 2004. It gives you get rich tones and hues in black and white. Red is the only colour for the copy. So that it jumps out.

This is a campaign in development. Subjects get reviewed every week. Since the positive campaign is running with the women's subjects for hope in future employment and equality, in the Ambush campaign we decide to bring in other burning women's issues. An urban middle-class housewife in a local bazaar lamenting about rising prices.

*A young girl standing in a bookshop and thinking about divisive politics. And how she does not adhere to it.*

*A father walking his son to school, unhappy with interference in textbooks.*

These get approved and shot at breakneck speed. This campaign runs till the end of elections.

They promised one crore jobs every year, but I am still waiting for one. Change your life. Change the government at the Centre.

They talk about bringing an education revolution but are distorting history books. Change your life. Change the government at the Centre.

They claim to have made a difference, but I only see the divide that they have created. Change your life. Change the government at the Centre.

Foreign companies are investing in India, but I lost my life's savings in the UTI scam. Change your life. Change the government at the Centre.

They say prices have come down, but why has my monthly budget increased? Change your life. Change the government at the Centre.

## APRIL 15, EVENING

For a change, most of us are in the agency. Ali and I are in a catch-up meeting in his room. He's constantly looking over his shoulders as if there is something happening outside. As I face the outside, I see Prantik walking very fast towards Ali's room. He bursts through the door and says, 'Ali, I just got a call from Priyanka Gandhi—she says the posters are very good and she wants the positives to be duplicated for her. We have to make a fresh set and she wants it today. Please tell someone to make the requisition.'

Poker-faced, Ali says, 'Oh, she called you?' He says, 'Yes my number is on all the printing proofs, so I am the central contact person on the job.'

Ali, still poker-faced: 'Wow, Prantik! So, you want to leave now to start the job?'

I am a bit baffled, but everything and anything is happening in these frenzied times. Just then, I see the crowd of young executives outside the door. Kabir, Vikram and Amit are watching this interaction, laughing. They burst into the room, to a very taken aback Prantik.

Now I get it. This is a prank!

They got one of the girls in the office to call and pretend to be PG. And Prantik got taken in. Obviously, Ali was part of the gang. Prantik is a great sport and we all have some light moments, some much-needed fun.

Back to work.

## APRIL 16

Anita Nayyar, Prince Khaneja and I are in a meeting. We are discussing finances, reconciling statements and checking on some nitty-gritties. Once this is done, I stay back to catch up with her. She tells me she was in a very late meeting last night with Voraji to get all the media approvals in. The newspaper list is over 250 and going through each paper and its editions with the client is a mind-bending job. The big challenge for the media department is scheduling. Which edition, in which state gets which ad? They have mapped the country with the problems in each state. Farmer suicides, the status of women, unemployment, etc. Accordingly, the emphasis is on which ad to publish.

The media plan printouts are long, really long. Endless. The material requisition sheet for each ad runs into pages. Ravi Negi, who works in Starcom, has to be very thorough while mapping this entire exercise. He has done a solid job of it.

## APRIL 18

ELECTION COMMISSION OF INDIA
Nirvachan Sadan, Ashoka Road, New Delhi - 110001
No. ECI/PN/17/2004 Dated: 18th April 2004
PRESS NOTE: The first Phase of polling for the General Election to the Lok Sabha will be held on 20th April, 2004. The polling will be held in 16 States/Union

Territories involving 140 parliamentary constituencies across the country. Election to the two PCs in Tripura will be held on 22-04-2004. 177614966 electors will exercise their right of franchise. The state-wise details of the number of polling stations, contesting candidates etc. are given in the enclosed statement. The Commission appeals to all voters to participate in large numbers to exercise their constitutional right to vote.

(S. K. KAURA) SECRETARY

# CHAPTER 16

## LITMUS TEST

## APRIL 20

Finally, it's happening. The first Phase of polling begins. Fingers crossed. Everyone is hoping for a 'not worse performance than last time'. In 1999, the Congress got 113 seats, the lowest ever in its history. Some opinion polls are pegging them at a measly 75 seats this time.

Around this time, I have to leave the country. I am on a senior management training programme and have to attend a workshop in Bali. I have already missed the first module in March which was also overseas. Could not travel due to the high pressure of this campaign at that time.

At our end, three campaigns are in progression, all in the creative execution stage. Ali, Rupam and teams are on the top of their game. It's running like a well-oiled machine. I decide to make the trip. Phone calls and SMS contact is always at hand.

I land in Singapore and switch on my phone. It's beeping non-stop with SMS on SMS. Lots of campaign-related updates from Ali, finance messages from Prince and so on. I stop to read some of them.

About the exit polls.

I can't believe what I'm reading on the tiny screen of my Nokia 6610. The exit polls are actually not bad. Nothing as scary as our worst nightmare of delivering less seats than last time.

On my connecting flight from Singapore to Bali, my mind is still in Delhi. Four months of complete madness, of almost drowning in the deep end many times, coming up for air and surviving the day, makes it hard for me to take in my new environment. And while I know everything will be fine, I also remain concerned about things.

## APRIL 26

The second Phase of polling begins.

The 2004 elections or the 14th general elections are historic. For the first time, two major alliances are fighting each other.

The main focus of the Congress and the BJP has been to woo political parties, especially the regional ones. The simple strategy of the two main national political parties is to contest alone in states where they have their own strong influence and to forge alliances in states where support would be required.

The BJP is solidifying existing alliances and scouting for new allies. It has maintained its alliance with strong regional political parties like the BJD in Odisha, Shiv Sena in Maharashtra, TDP in Andhra Pradesh, JD(U) in Bihar and Meghalaya, SAD in Punjab and has added MNF in Mizoram, the SDF in Sikkim, IFDP in Kerala, the NPF in Nagaland and AIADMK in place of the DMK in Tamil Nadu. In Arunachal Pradesh, Assam, Delhi, Goa, Gujarat, Haryana, Himachal Pradesh, J&K, Jharkhand, Karnataka, Kerala, Madhya Pradesh, Manipur, Rajasthan, Uttar Pradesh and Uttarakhand, the party decided to contest alone because of its dominating presence.

Their manifesto was released on 8 April. They seem very confident. Preponing the elections by eight months, the huge wins in December in three states, the feel-good factor, the Bharat Uday rath yatra of LK Advani, state-of-the-art technology and modern war rooms, 'India Shining' running continuously since October 2003, makes them feel they are on a winning wicket.

They give out seven pillars of governance, if elected back to power.

The Congress party so far has been averse to alliances to fight elections. In her presidential address on 8 November at the Mount Abu conclave, Sonia Gandhi advised her party to prepare for the 2004 elections. For the first time, she declared coalitions would not be ruled out and that like-minded parties could come together to fight as the opposition. She stated that all secular parties should fight for retaining non-communalism.

The defeats in December spurred the thought of forming a secular alliance. On 28 December 2003, on the founding day of the party in Mumbai, she announced this. This was reinforced on 13 February 2004 when Pranab Mukherjee's report on the Congress defeats in December 2003 was tabled. It clearly gave the direction of a win happening only with alliances and not alone.

The Congress forged alliances in Tamil Nadu, Andhra Pradesh, Kerala, Maharashtra and Bihar with DMK, TRS, Muslim League, NCP and RJD respectively.

## APRIL 26, NIGHT

Exit polls are all over the news.

They are predicting that the NDA is losing steam. That there will be a hung Lok Sabha!

Our teams are glued to prime time news. I'm getting text messages from everyone. Like a ball-by-ball commentary. All of us are feeling a mutual excitement but not showing it. Still another two phases of polling to go. Just half the country is done till now and, anyway, the last Phase on May 10 is the single largest polling day.

Let's wait, we tell ourselves.

I return to the heat and dust of the capital.

The next few days go by in the same daze. The campaign is chugging along full throttle and the team is busy.

## END-APRIL

One night, waiting for a meeting to begin, I think to myself how much we as a team we have grown. We are in and out of offices and residences of erstwhile ministers. Everyone is dealing confidently and maturely. From the beginning, I had told everyone to treat them like normal clients. This is a brand we are launching or let's put it correctly, relaunching. That's it. That is the one-word brief to the team. Walk tall. Be firm. Be cool. And I feel most people in the agency are liked by the client. They seem professional, work-oriented.

As for me—am just that. Talk to the point. Fight for what I believe in and argue when required. As a leader, I am a firm believer that a good environment is what people thrive in and for their best to emerge I have to create that work climate. And that I will have their back no matter what. I have looked at myself as a person who goes to work. Never a woman. Except when it comes to dicey toilets!

Ali is forever cracking jokes and has a poker face at all times. What's going on in his head is a different matter altogether. His being very good in English and Hindi have helped us with the job tremendously. Always observing.

Rupam has his own brand of fun. He loves teasing people and is very observant. A great leader of his team and quick to firefight. During this campaign, he has a special book. With large sheets of paper. He draws out each piece of work so that art direction is clear and production work is clear.

A thought crosses my mind. Suddenly, out of the blue.

I tell them both why don't we do a concluding ad. One that collates everything, clears the reforms and development issues once and for all.

We brainstorm ideas there and then.

Next day by lunch it's ready. An almost full-page newspaper advertisement in colour with the very bold font headline: *Kisne kiya kaam aur kisne jataya naam?*

Below the headline are boxes like a survey, giving each achievement and the multiple-choice answers: Congress. Others.

Things like

Who made IIT, IIM?
Green Revolution
Industries
Telecom

Clearly emphasising the growth issues and reforms issues. And the visual has a multitude of real Indian faces representing different religions. Clearly endorsing secularism. Tolerance for all.

In the agency, this ad gets christened as *The tick ad*. Pooja and the creatives have a term for it. Jayshree's ad.

I decide to go and present it myself. I believe it will give added impetus to the campaign. Especially now that the exit polls were not negative at all. If people are losing faith in 'India Shining', it's time to show them which party they could put their faith in.

Jairam and Salman are at South Avenue. It's crowded as usual. Jairam is in his tiny little room, working on his laptop, usually listening to western classical music. He joins the meeting in the main room. They add a few boxes to tick, clearly where our understanding is not so deep. They brainstorm on the headline. It actually gets crafted in the meeting.

Anita has also come along for the meeting. We request them to give it a strong release. Across the states where the last two phases of polling are still due. The advertisement is in what we call a 'page robber' size. Not big enough to fill the page (therefore less expensive than a full-page size) and large enough for no other ad to be accommodated on that page. They agree in principle.

Who did all the work, and who walked away with the credit? You decide!

Luckily, Rupam and Pooja have shot people of different faiths. Now she will have to create a proper collage out of it.

This ad gets ready. It starts appearing close to the polling date.

## MAY 6

Third Phase of polling for the 2004 Lok Sabha elections.

The same discussions are carrying on. The voices are getting louder. NDA will form the government, is the rhetoric people have got used to. They are all saying it on repeat mode with perhaps a few making a concession for Congress for improving its position from the December no-show.

## MAY 10

The last Phase of polling.

Minor fact. It's also my birthday. There's a call on my phone. I am wondering if it's the client and what could they want now. But its brother dearest Probir from Dubai. He wishes me and tells me he is intently following the political scenario in India. A few days to the results.

We dress up and head for the polling booth. Casting my vote this time feels utterly strange.

It's Monday. I head to the office. Ma is still in Delhi. Thank God. My crazy schedules have grounded her here. It's blazing hot. Schools have shut down for the summer.

# CHAPTER 17

## ROLE REVERSAL

SO FAR, THE client has never been to our office. The confidentiality clause of our agreement has worked 100 per cent. Now that the polls are over, it's time to invite them over. We hope they accept. Of course, they do. They tell us they will come by 3 pm.

Our team decides to make an occasion out of it. A small group gets together and plans this out. A huge 5-kg cake is ordered in the hand shape. It has the line 'Congress *ko LB mila.*'

The box in which it arrives is huge. Three or four men carry it in. Madhu is in charge.

Rupam has come out with a great idea for their personal gifts. He organises table-size easels and does individual caricatures for each of them. Their quirks and statements and looks picked up over the last five months. They have come out very well. We all have a laugh as we see them. They are packed in nice gift bags.

At 3 pm, they arrive. Salman Khurshid, Jairam Ramesh, Shamim, Vibhakar Shastri.

They are taken to the conference room and, finally, a relaxed thirty minutes are spent talking about the incidents of the last four-and-a-half months. There is laughter on shared anecdotes. The snacks plate reminds me of the pitch day. It's pretty much the same teatime fare. Samosas, sandwiches and chips along with tea. Pramod and Raju from the canteen are doing their best, albeit nervous. The counting of votes is the next day. We are all making guesses. Even though the exit polls are not fully negative and in fact have been encouraging. There is still a sense of mixed feelings. Part excitement, part fear, part worry.

Fingers crossed as everyone is quietly wishing it's no worse than the debacle of 1999. That's the whisper going around.

Madhu from admin walks in and asks if we can come outside. The client team don't have a clue about the cake. As we all troop outside, there is this big 'hand cake' in the centre of the office. We all surround it. The entire office is present. The cake is cut by Ramesh and Khurshid amidst claps and cheers. Someone calls for a speech. Salman Khurshid makes a very nice speech. It's full of praise for the agency. He lists out the effort and says it was a wonderful partnership, whatever may be the result.

This is met with resounding claps. Of course, everyone's eyes are on the cake. A 5-kg cake is devoured in no time.

Time for them to leave. They have spent over an hour with us. The first hour in our association where no work was discussed.

Wonder what's in store the next day.

It's 6 pm. For the first time since January 6, I leave the office on time.

9 pm. Primetime news is full of noise and excitement. News anchors and expert psephologists are waxing eloquent

on their theories. The TV screen is full of bar charts and pie charts. There is huge anticipation for the results the next day. Counting days are always exciting.

The exit polls have given their verdict.

The NDTV-AC Nielsen exit poll predicts 230-250 seats for the NDA and 190-205 for the Congress, while others are expected to get 100-120 seats.

The Aaj Tak ORG-MARG exit poll is giving NDA 248 seats and Congress 190, while predicting 105 for the others.

The Star News C-Voter survey predicts 263-275 for NDA, 174-186 for Congress, and 86-98 to others.

Tomorrow, by lunch time, it will be clear if these trends are correct.

The messages on our phone are quiet. Think the team is already asleep. It's been a long long first-half of the year. Like three years packed in one.

# CHAPTER 18

## RESULTS DAY

## MAY 13

The newspapers have arrived. They state that more than 1 million Electronic Voting Machines (EVM) were used in all 543 parliamentary constituencies in the country. This is the first time this is happening. A first for the Indian voting system. The old-style ballot boxes have been replaced.

It's a hot and dry day in Delhi. I decide to stay home and watch the results. Whatever it may be, the comfort of home is where I want to be. All the members on the agency team are in their respective homes as well. Everything is quiet.

Phones have been silent since the morning. Either people are still sleeping or too tired and tense.

I put on the TV and stay in my room. The results will trickle in through the morning. Flipping channels through the first few minutes, I see most of the client team we have dealt with, at different studios of the news channels. Hindi, English, Tamil and Bengali channels are what I am changing swiftly on my remote.

It's about 45 minutes into the telecast. I rush out and call in Ma and Tarini. Something seems to be happening. I can't believe my eyes. The bar charts and pie charts and arrows and symbols on the screen are showing Congress leading in many seats. Do I see correctly? Ma puts on her spectacles and assures me I see right. Tarini is young but she gets into the mood.

I look at my phone. There are messages from Kosty and Rupam. 'Is this real?' they both are asking.

No message from Ali. I call him up repeatedly. His voice sounds groggy. I tell him to turn on the news.

Anita calls. 'What is going on?'

Prince calls.

Prantik calls.

Pooja messages. Jasbir messages.

Arvind calls.

And the counting continues. Sonia Gandhi wins by a huge margin. So, do many many of her colleagues. It's crossed the 113 mark now. Phew! Better than 1999.

A lot of counting is still to be done. The incumbent party is not getting as many seats as was predicted for them by all the exit polls.

What finally happens is unbelievable.

Sonia Gandhi's Congress wins 219 out of 539 seats for which votes were counted today in the 543-member Lok Sabha! That's the result if we are to state it in one line.

And, finally, it's over!

No single party won the absolute majority of 272 seats.

As they say, it takes two hands to clap. The energy to win started galvanising from the client's end from March 2004. The rallies, quick turnarounds, approvals, execution, availability for meetings and calls at all odd hours put an added *josh* into the response from the agency.

## THE RESULTS

| | 1999 | 2004 |
|---|---|---|
| Ruling Alliance (led by Bhartiya Janata Party) | 298 | 185 |
| *Bhartiya Janata Party by itself* | *182* | *137* |
| Congress + Allies | 135 | 220 |
| *Congress by itself* | *112* | *145* |
| Left-wing Parties | 42 | 63 |

# CHAPTER 19

## ADVERTISING WORKS

EUPHORIA AT THE Congress headquarters. At 10 Janpath. All across the country. The streets are full of Congress workers and supporters dancing and rejoicing with abandon. This is an astounding victory. No one had given them a chance.

Our client has emerged as the single largest party in the Lok Sabha elections. And with their pre-poll alliances, they have 219 seats. With the 63 seats of the Left parties who joined hands to support the Congress party from outside, they formed the government. Thus, was born the United Progressive Alliance.

This has been a victory of sheer hard work and grit and determination. An upset. The true epitome of David and Goliath. Perhaps something to be said about the opposing party peaking too early? But more than that it was about who got the strategy right. Who understood the consumer better, and who reached the heart and the mind equally?

The underdog coming from out of the woods and winning?

They can't get over it.

Our phones are buzzing. We are all calling each other in disbelief and joy and relief.

The country too has lived through a historic win. Where the voice of the people counted. It witnessed the biggest relaunch of a brand. A brand which strengthened its salience and relevance. Once again in 2004 after almost a decade. And my team and I did play a part in it.

If there is a case study to prove that advertising works, this is it.

I rest my case.

ON MAY 16, there was a meeting at 10 Janpath. All the coalition partners were present and jubilant and wanted Madam Gandhi to be the PM. The SP and BSP also were supporting the Congress from outside.

On the 18th, she declined the post citing personal reasons. Of course, she continued as President of the Congress Parliamentary Party and Chairperson of the UPA.

On the 19th, Dr Manmohan Singh was designated Prime Minister.

All these parties put together formed what was named the United Progressive Alliance. They called us to design the logo and the booklet of the Common Minimum Programme which was the charter of UPA 1. When we went to present the creatives at South Avenue it seemed like a different era. In just one week, so much had changed. Everything was quiet again. The canteen boy served tea with his forever sweet attitude, the logo and booklet got approved at the first shot and we drove back quietly.

I pass the little house sometimes, diagonally opposite Teen Murti Bhavan and gaze at it. It's silent and benign. But the walls know what madness took place there in January-May 2004.

As far as our team went, we were an understated bunch. On the 14th, there was a lot of back-slapping and joy in the office. Utter happiness. Arvind called and said we would celebrate the next time he came. I had a small request for him. How about giving an out-of-turn spot bonus to everyone in the office—those who were on the Congress team and those who weren't. Because the second lot kept the other business going without too many issues. He agreed. These were token amounts. But as they were a surprise, they were received with total happiness.

- Ali recovered and started talking normally by the end of June. His poker face remained intact as the funniest wisecracks returned.
- Rupam promised to cook an Assamese meal and treat us to a good dinner. Job meetings in his room continued.
- Anita bought herself another ring, she finally got the time.
- Prince and the finance department rested their hands after writing thousands of cheques.
- Prantik rushed to handle a major launch which was delayed due to this client.
- Kosty, Pooja, Sanjiv and the rest in creative blared music louder and ordered a good Thai meal.
- Kabir, Amit, Vikram and the rest of the executives took their bikes out for a joy ride.
- Jasbir got rid of the shredder and additional fax machine which crunched her sitting space.
- The studio artists and canteen staff chilled a bit.

- The admin department wondered what to do with the secret room.
- Madhu continued buying apples and the reception was always welcoming.
- The guards and riders slept properly after almost five months.

As for me. I thought back to that morning of 6 January, when I presumed a friend was fooling me. The nerves of delivering a good year. Of entering the big league in the Delhi market.

So, what next?

While the lives of a billion Indians changed at the country level, in our own beautiful colourful office everything changed. We won an account every month till the rest of the year and beyond. All clients wanted the team that had worked on the Congress. We became a formidable force in the Delhi market. Our client list got bigger names and we won many accolades.

Why did I choose to tell this story so many years later? Simply because it had to be told. From many points of views.

To prove once again that advertising works. Living and working on one of the greatest case studies in India and not telling the story would be a disservice to the profession that is the most exciting, creative, frustrating, strategic, fun—in other words, the best.

To everyone who loves history and politics, this is a story for you. This year marked the coming of age of political brands— Where both major competitors worked with professional agencies.

To all MBA students, an inspiring case study for your bed-time reading. And also, some key learnings. Essentially to know the power of winning ideas, research, hard work and not giving up.

To anyone who likes stories like the phoenix rising from the ashes, underdogs and David Goliath tales, well here is a real-life example.

And lastly, like India, this was a story of youth. Ninety per cent of our team was under 34 to India's 74 per cent.

And while I was in the 10 per cent of the team age-wise, as a woman leading this effort, I was perhaps less than one per cent of the workforce in that position, at least in Delhi. So, to all the young girls out there—believe in yourself.

## POSTSCRIPT

RAHUL GANDHI AND Priyanka Vadra wrote very nice messages to me for the agency, post the victory

Sonia Gandhi sent me a lovely letter when we won Agency of the Year in 2005.

*The Economic Times* rated '*Congress ka haath aam aadmi ke saath*' among the top six Indian political slogans of all times.

*Business Today* rated it as the 'top marketing campaign of 2004'.

The term *Aam aadmi* acquired a life of its own. A web series with that name, people's Twitter handle calling themselves 'mango men' and interestingly, a political party's name too. Perhaps it is all a coincidence!

# A FRACTION OF THE MEDIA COVERAGE

## MEDIA PLANNERS SAY BJP'S MUCH-TOUTED CAMPAIGN BACKFIRED

# Blame It On 'India Shining'

**NIVEDITA MOOKERJI**
*New Delhi*

Media planners close to the Congress camp attributed the success of the party to its "bang-on" campaign. Those tracking the BJP slide said that the party lacked compelling mass media campaigns. The apolitical industry pundits, on the other hand, claimed that campaigns only have a limited impact on elections. Interestingly, media insiders, in general, argued that the NDA government's 'India Shining' campaign backfired. Political advertising cost the parties a total of around Rs 250 crore, as per estimates. Add to that at least another Rs 100 crore on 'India Shining' and 'Bharat Uday' campaigns, though there's no clarity on these figures yet.

Starcom executive director Anita Nayyar. Advertising and media campaign is among those factors, she said. When asked to elaborate on the strategy behind the Congress campaign, Ms Nayyar told FE: "It's bang-on, talking to aam admi." She added: "The Congress focussed on real issues." These issues, according to her, included how common people were untouched by the BJP feel-good policies.

Another media insider, Mr Sushil Pandit, who's director, The Hive, felt that "the Congress campaign was not terrific", but admitted that "BJP could have done with a better media campaign". The party should have showcased compelling reasons in its mass media campaigns as to why BJP should be brought back to

BJP started quite late on its campaign and political advertising. Congress got a lead of about one month in its mass-media campaign, according to Mr Pandit. "BJP shot itself in the foot as far as media campaign goes. The party failed to capitalise on the positives. There was just no cohesion in sending the right message across to the voters. The messages kept changing, leaving the BJP in a disarray," he said.

Universal McCann president Chintamani Rao, who's been away from the country for a few weeks, missed the final round of political ads/campaigns. But, Mr Rao said that media campaigns have only a limited reach. Newspaper campaigns are read only by the educated few. Similarly, political ads on cable

explained. (There are 45 million cable TV homes and a total of around 100 million TV homes in the country.) So, Mr Rao believes that media campaigns don't have much of an impact on how election results could swing.

Commenting on NDA government's 'India Shining' campaign, Ms Nayyar said it didn't touch the common man and that its after-effect was not good. According to Mr Rao, this campaign targeted only the urban middle class. And Mr Pandit felt "India Shining was bit of an overkill and towards the end, it turned counter-productive."

Summing up the impact of media campaigns on the election results, Mr Pandit said: "BJP was complacent." It's hard to tell whether the "clumsiness" of the party's media

Financial Express, 14 May 2004.-

The Times of India - Masthead - May 14th 2004

The Economic Times, Masthead, May 14th 2004

# Aam Aadmi campaign is here to stay: Congress

**By Ratna Bhushan**
TIMES NEWS NETWORK

**New Delhi:** Election fever may be over and done with, but the hype doesn't seem to be ebbing.

The resounding — and unexpected — success that the Congress party's *Aam Aadmi ko kya mila* low-budget campaign met with, has the party asking for more.

In a move that could set a benchmark for political advertising in India, the Congress has decided to stretch the equity of the *Aam Aadmi* message even after the elections through its ad agency Leo Burnett.

The *Aam Aadmi* message is being taken forward, and this will be done in three stages, informs Congress leader Salman Khurshid.

The first element will be conventional advertising in the mass media — TV and print — highlighting the achievements of the party. 'Several messages in our campaign got lost because of too much advertising happening prior to the elections.

We plan to replay some of those messages and slogans linked with specific events," says Khurshid.

Second, the Congress website, currently in English

**Reaching out to masses**

and Hindi, will be re-launched and set up in Urdu to begin with, followed by other languages with the underlying message of *Aam Aadmi.*

Finally, there's a move to network party members by making use of smart cards carrying the *Aam Aadmi* messages, says Khurshid.

Says Jayshree Sundar, executive director, Leo Burnett: "This is the coming of age of political advertising — much like it happens in the West. It is about treating a political party as a brand backed by complex and scientific media scheduling."

The Congress has not yet taken a call on the budgets to be allocated to this sustained communication exercise.

The four-month *Congress ka haath, Aam Aadmi ke saath* campaign was done on a budget of about Rs 20 crore across mass media with a specific target audience of unemployed youth, small investors, farmers and women.

While electronic and radio advertising were released in nine languages, press advertisements were done in 11 languages.

In contrast, BJP's Rs 65-crore elitist India Shining communication package included SMS messages, phone calls and hoardings.

The Bhartiya Janata Party's LK Advani recently admitted that 'feel good' and 'India Shining' backfired on the party.

Times of India, 2004.

The Brand Reporter, June 1-15, 2004

## Brand
### FEATURE

ELECTION CAMPAIGNING | Congress

# Khadi meets powerpoint

Utpal Bhaskar

Electoral campaigning in India underwent a sea change this year. The 14th Lok Sabha elections witnessed a more systematic use of media than ever before and welter of money being spent. The Indian media has never had it so good.

In one corner was the Bharatiya Janata Party, represented by Grey Worldwide, and on the other, the Congress with Leo Burnett handling the account. According to data supplied by Adex India, a division of TAM Media Research, close to Rs 175 crore was collectively spent by all the parties put together between January and May 2004, in trying to woo over 670 million people who elected 539 representatives.

The advertising war is a study in contrasts. To counter the BJP's glossy, feel-good advertising, the Congress campaign tried to reach out to the poor rural voters who were less than enthusiastic about India's recent economic growth. Burnett used 'commercials' shot in a gritty, cinema verite style.

TAM data says that the BJP outspent the Congress more than 2:1 on press and TV. The ruling party blew up Rs 52.4 crore as compared to the Congress' Rs 13.4 crore. BJP's Rs 30.1 crore TV budget was spent mostly on mainstream channels, including ZEE News, STAR Plus and Sony. The top channels targeted by the Congress campaign were STAR Plus followed by Sony and ZEE. The party spent Rs 1.8 crore on regional channels such as Udaya TV, Alpha Gujarati, Maa TV and Alpha Marathi, in sync with the party's communication strategy of reaching out to the 'other India' in their languages.

The Congress spent Rs 15.8 crore – or about two thirds of its budget – in print whereas the BJP's Rs 22.3 crore constituted only about 40 per cent of its total spend. In press advertising Congress spent Rs 15.8 crore as compared to BJP's Rs 22.3 crore. The top three publications targeted by the Congress in terms of spends were The Times Of India, India Today and Hindustan Times. Press ads in Samyukta, Deccan Herald, Gujarat Samachar and Daily Sakal

maintained the regional presence for the party. The top two publications targeted by the BJP in terms of spends were the Chattisgarh editions of Dainik Bhaskar and Navbharat Times.

Leo Burnett bagged the Congress fairly late in the day, on February 19, at a time when BJP's 'India Shining' campaign was at its peak. "The only way left to us was to talk about real issues, tough issues and honest issues," says Jayshree Sundar, executive director, Leo Burnett, Delhi. The Congress campaign was led by creative director Rupam Borah and vice president Ali Imran,

along with a dedicated team at Delhi, with support from Leo Burnett, Mumbai.

The first stop for the agency was to prioritise the goals of the campaign. Maharashtra, Andhra Pradesh, Karnataka, Gujarat, Chattisgarh, Rajasthan, Punjab and Delhi were chettypicked to maximise impact. The agency used different creatives for the north and the south. The campaign was led from small towns and district headquarters rather than from the metros.

'Congress ka haath' shifted from 'garib' (poor) to 'aam aadmi' (common man). 'Congress ke haath, aam aadmi ke saath'

became the campaign mantra. The campaign strategically focused on the vernacular dailies keeping in mind that a large percentage of the country's population doesn't speak, let alone read English. "We were aggressive at the right moments. We suggested our client talk like a leader as people welcome a certain degree of control," says Sundar.

The party spent about 80-90 per cent of the total budget on rural media. The campaign broke in three phases in sync with the four-phased election process. In the first phase, which began from March 2, it talked

about 'Aam aadmi ke dya sukh' (what did the common man get?). This was the issue raised leg. Three films and five radio spots in nine languages were used at this stage. The 180-sr press ads in 11 languages talked about unemployment, problems faced by farmers and criticised the advertising blitzkrieg of BJP as a royal waste of the tax payer's money. This was followed up with ads talking about the communal divide and the various warrs of the BJP era.

The second phase of the Congress campaign was branded the 'achievement campaign'. At this stage, the ads shifted focus to

the strides made during the earlier Congress regime – including the establishment of the Panchayat Raj, India gaining the status of a nuclear power, industrial revolution and the party's farmer-friendly policies.

The third phase, or the 'vision campaign', talked about what the future could be like under Congress. At this stage, the party used television and press and included impact features in Telugu, Hindi and English. Its posters in 11 languages portrayed female power, communal harmony, new employment avenues and Sonia Gandhi's persona. Cartoon ads and SMS messaging were also included.

Every now and then the thrust and parry turned ugly. BJP supporters ran ads challenging Sonia Gandhi's commitment to India by pointing out that she was born an Italian. An independent ad backing the Congress suggested that Prime Minister Vajpayee had been a British influence. The whole exercise, conceived and executed in three months flat, was a logistical nightmare, dealt with the issues that were changing constantly but Sundar says that "Congress was an outstanding client."

In an election, it is hard to gauge how much of a role advertising had in the outcome because of the vast variety of factors at play in a short period of time. In spite of the surprise result, the fact is that at a national level, both the Congress and the BJP saw a swing of about 2 per cent away from themselves. In retrospect, there is a view that the India Shining campaign may have been overdone. Girish Chandrashekhar, vice president and general manager, McCann Erickson, Chennai, voices a common opinion, "The Congress campaign was not as overpowering as BJP's India Shining campaign. India Shining was a good theme but the strategy was wrong. It became too metro-centric."

Professional spin masters are relatively new players in Indian elections, which have been traditionally won on the back of grassroots campaigning, rallies and speeches about national policies and local issues. This election wasn't the first in which politicians used multi-media advertising. Still, it is easy to see how sharply its role is growing in each election. ●

Sundar: "the only way left for us was to talk about real issues"

# The BJP and its middle course

By Neena Vyas

NEW DELHI, AUG. 2. Caught between the call of the Sangh Parivar and the threat of the National Democratic Alliance crumbling if it were to return to a "hard Hindutva" path, the Bharatiya Janata Party seems to have decided, for the moment, to take a middle course at its 'chintan baithak' that concluded its indoor-day session in Goa today.

Summing up the discussions between the party's 30-odd top leaders in a "10-point conclusions" paper, the BJP said it would "focus on ideological orientation" even as it makes efforts to strengthen and expand its base while "continuing to work with its allies" in the NDA.

## Twin commitments

There is hardly any doubt that the Rashtriya Swayamsevak Sangh and a section of the party, led by the Leader of the Opposition, L.K. Advani, has been

### NEWS ANALYSIS

insisting that the future of the BJP lies in adopting Hindutva even if under the different name of "nationalism", as opposed to the former Prime Minister, Atal Bihari Vajpayee's "development" plank. For the moment, the party simply stated that nationalism and development will be its "twin commitments", inseparable from each other.

It appears that the veiled threat held out by the Janata Dal (United) that it would have to rethink its tie-up with the BJP if the latter decided to embrace again the contentious issues it had put on the backburner for the last six years did have a salutary effect on the "chintan baithak".

While the word "Hindutva" was missing in the document, it approved committed as "integral humanism" of Deen Dayal Upadhyaya and "nationalism as an ideology." The document vowed to restore the "the primacy of ideology and idealism" at all levels in the party and work hard to ensure a smooth relationship between the party and the "nationalist organisations."

What emerged is a two-fold political strategy. One, to sharpen Hindutva and the other, to change the image of the BJP from that of a party of the urban rich and the upwardly mobile to that which has its feet firmly planted in poor and rural India. Under the first plan, the party would take up mass campaigns on several issues which would clearly serve to polarise society along communal lines — the document mentioned campaigns against reservations for Muslims (as announced by the Andhra Government but stayed by the courts), the alarming rise in "jehadi terrorism" and the "competitive pseudo-secularism" of the Congress and the Left. Curiously, the party also talked about winning over the minorities. Conscious that the Vajpayee Government had followed policies such as giving subsidies for Haj, the party is now planning to explain to its cadre "what is appeasement [of the minorities] and what is not."

## 'Voice of farmers'

Under the second point of its two-fold plan, it would campaign against the "anti-poor, anti-farmer, anti-worker and anti-rural" policies of the United Progressive Alliance Government. It would seem this has emerged from the results of the Lok Sabha election and the perception that the Congress was effectively able to portray itself as the party of the "aam admi" (the common man), which cared for the poor farmer and the impoverished rural areas of the country. It also re-flected the BJP's desire to expand its political base. It has talked about taking up issues such as "scarcity of water" and finding ways to make the BJP the authentic "voice of farmers."

Over the next three months, these issues will be discussed threadbare taking the "Task Ahead" paper, presented at the Mumbai national executive committee meeting, as the working paper and giving it a concrete shape.

The Hindu, August 3.

Professional spin-masters are new players in Indian elections, which traditionally have been won through grass-roots campaigns featuring rallies punctuated by speeches about macroeconomic policies and local issues. This election wasn't the first where politicians used advertisements. Still, it did mark the first time Indian political parties planned national ad campaigns that drew from corporate-branding strategies.

Total political ad spending for the parties increased 40% since the last elections in 1999, according to TAM Media Research, a Bombay media research firm. In the process, TV emerged as an important campaign medium, as cable reached more and more households. "The advertising helped because it started debate. People enjoyed the campaign as entertainment -- they gave soaps a run for their money," says McCann's Mr. Joshi.

Wall Street journal 14th May 2004.

# Good doc says no to glam-shows

## Aam Admi Is Manmohan Singh's Latest Obsession

By Shankar Roy/TNN

New Delhi: It's like reaping his own purse. The good doc who was once in thrall for selfies among CEOs, investment experts, stock market pundits and fellow economists, has said no to the glitzy and glam things of life.

Take for example the international conference on space scheduled to be held in Bangalore later this month. Despite the high profile of the event and significant American participation, Manmohan Singh has conveyed his inability to mark his presence there. Reason: the PM will be busy working on his rural reconstruction plans. For the same reason, he turned down a request recently to take part in the Olympic flame relay in the Capital. He has taken the common minimum programme of the government seriously and at the moment is completely obsessed with its implementation, said a close aide.

As if to make a point, Singh will preside over a function of the rural development ministry soon — his first public programme outside the routine political activity and official work.

Unable to speak in Parliament during the debate on the motion of thanks to the President's address in case of disruptions by the opposition, the PM is going to address his fellow countrymen on television. But let there be no curiosity about a possible 20% echo; this aides guess Singh will perhaps speak in Hindi for the most part of his speech since he is keen to communicate to the aam admi.

He is likely to talk about the promise of implementing well-meaning programmes for the common man with adequate attention because of the flawed delivery system. The man who, as fi nance minister, made terms like market and reform house-hold words has now zeroed in on the other end — ensuring by the number of rural meetings with fi nance minister Chidambaram and some old buddies from the overseeing departments, he is discussing the ways of reviving the farm sector.

"He is doing meticulous homework," an aide says, pointing out that apart from the fi rst cabinet meeting on security, he has mostly discussed with his cabinet colleagues issues which were considered un-fashionable until the other day — agriculture, animal husbandry, water and food security.

There is a lurking suspicion that at this rate the Marxists, who once accused him in Parliament for seeking the warming machine cheaper, will soon call him Comrade Singh.

---

# Aam aadmi ko kya mila? Rs 19,228 cr for rural areas

The importance of rural development at the annual review of the ministry of rural development for 2005-06 has been released recently. The report has given a push of the importance in the fi elds of work, employment, infrastructure and welfare, apart from other programmes in various sectors.

The budgetary outlay for rural development last year was the highest ever, over and above with the Rs 1,114 crore made available. Much of the expansion was the special component of the bargaining Gramin Rozgar Yojana (SGRY) through which employment was provided to minority-affected areas of the country. For 2006-07, a budget provision of Rs 19,128 crore has been made. For infrastructure the Bharat Nirman project is the drinking water sector and Barraj initiative is watershed management and habitation and the corpus that would compound.

The social and new government's agenda have focused about Rs 45,000 crore in rural drinking water supply schemes of 2005-06 over the last four years. Much emphasis highlighted on the Clean over 30% of rural water sector schemes including rural plan, aside the parameters over time. This will know about 19.4

ROAD TO WELL-BEING

RURAL MURAL

integrated watershed development programme. Under the Pradhan Mantri Gram Sadak Yojana, during 2005-06, 18,448 habitations were covered under another additional 6,619 road works. Rs 5,533 crore were 30 states being cleared in the last fi nancial year. Under the Indira Awaas Yojana, the fl agship scheme of the rural housing programme, 16 lakh SC/ST/Minority beneficiaries were assisted as proposed in the current year.

Coming to the health sector, under the total sanitation drive assured over 108 districts, 68 lakh individual latrines, 52,688 school toilets, about 6,000 sanitary complexes and 1,640 rural sanitary marts and production units have been constructed.

In employment, since the inception of SGRY, 20,723 lakh man-days of work has been created and a percentage of the 18,468 crore under this fund has been generated from nearly towards higher figures since inception in 2006 and until March this year 19,128 lakh with help given have been created. A total of 46 lakh man-days have been assisted with the latest figures for 22,227 assisted under the schemes 16,127 crore works allotted and Rs 6.343 crore work created from inception.

ASIAN Age Consultants/ESG

---

# Kahani ghar ghar ki: MPs want to be aam aadmi

## Housing Panel Chief Hooda Has Legislators Lined Up For VIP Bungalows In Lutyen's Zone

Ramesh Kumar

SShhhh... HE'S AN MP

---

Aam aadmi phrase gaining currency.

# India's Best Marketers

W HAT DO A 118-YEAR-OLD POLITICAL PARTY, a Bollywood production house, an upstart (and start-up) low-cost airline, the initial public offering of a biotech company and the entire off-shoring-to-India trend have in common? Well, according to a panel of judges BT put together, they marketed themselves or their offerings best in 2004. The result, detailed in the pages that follow, is the second edition of *Business Today's* Best Marketers. Like the first edition, this was based on an expert interview with specialists (think consultants, academics, researchers) across six centres: Delhi, Mumbai, Hyderabad, Chennai, Bangalore and Kolkata. As they met these specialists (around three in each centre), our reporters discovered something strange; unlike last year, when the judges came up with a total of 13 names, this time, the number of entries common across them was a mere five. One way of looking at that is to surmise that the quality of marketing has dipped. Another (the one we prefer) is that these five marketers have done enough to be obvious choices.

Air Deccan

The Congress Party

Yash Raj Films

Biocon

Indian IT

## Congress

# Hoi Polloi Hosannas

**Forget what it did for its image; the Congress' advertising and marketing campaign successfully repositioned the Bharatiya Janata Party as an urban clique.**

THE MARKETING SUCCESS story of the year was scripted by a 118-year-old brand that most people had written off: the Congress Party. Thus, when it was announced late last year that elections to the 14th Lok Sabha would be held in April and May, 2004, no one gave the Congress a chance. The incumbent Bharatiya Janata Party (BJP)-led National Democratic Alliance (NDA) embarked on a crore-crore-plus India Shining (and hey, we made it shine) campaign. That gave the Congress some ammunition: rather than waste its energies and margin resources on positioning itself—not easy at all, especially given the fact that it had been out of power for nine years and, no matter what its modest wonks now claim, not very sure of what it stood for—it decided to reposition the BJP, as Harsh Verma, a marketing lecturer at Faculty of Management Studies, New Delhi, puts it: "as a party meant for the urban upper crust elite." The advertising strategy that the party chose, then, says Jamboree bundat, Executive Director, Leo Burnett, the agency that created this in-now legendary Congress ka Haath, Aam Aadmi ke Saath (the chosen insolubility would be, the hand of the Congress is always there

to help the common man; in equal parts, a vision statement and a play on the party's election symbol, the hand) campaign, "was about relevance and relatability." "We did not make the mistake of thinking everybody above 18 was equal," she adds. Nor did the party make the erroneous assumption that India is one market. Its advertisements, 3,600 of them spread over 60 days, appeared in 32 languages. "We ran a regional campaign," says Jairam Ramesh, the brains behind the campaign and now a member of the Rajya Sabha. "Not a national campaign translated into a regional one." The party's marketing effort itself was broken into four phases; the first was seven days of intensive demolition of the NDA's India Shining campaign; the second, 10 days spent highlighting the Congress' achievements; the third, 15 days spent outlining the party's vision; and the last three devoted to the kind of hysterical hyperbole without which no party conceives its marketing campaign. "We actually depicted Vajpayee (Atal Bihari Vajpayee, the former Prime Minister of the country and a BJP leader) as Ravana," chortles a gleeful Ramesh.

None of this addressed the problem the Congress faced. The party, says Santosh Desai,

President, McCann Erickson India, an advertising agency, "has always occupied this core (thin, liberal), mostly sort of space", and to manage, even after close to six months to offer (as the largest party in the United Progressive Alliance government), is on "its centreline". What it did do was to take on the India Shining campaign head on and ask, as it did, Aam aadmi ke liye roti (what has the state on this urban gentry got to show?). Along the way, the party discovered a new and saleable brand ambassador in its President Sonia Gandhi—her presence, concedes McCann's Desai, "has given the Congress some guiding principle where it earlier had none"—who let the campaign end with a vengeance in a sort of below-the-bar one-to-one marketing effort. "The Congress comeback is a marketing success story," says Nirvik Singh, Chairman (South Asia), Grey Worldwide, the agency behind the India Shining ads, although he is quick to add that "ads are not the only things that matter in politics; a lot of other things come into play". Else they do, and the Congress, as is evident from the fact that it is the leading constituent of the alliance that governs India today, was ahead on these too.

— SMARJEET SINGH

**At the beginning of the year the Congress boasted 114 seats in the Lok Sabha; today, it does 145**

# Hand In A Velvet Glove

**The Congress swept the polls with a simple strategy: "Think global, act local." Brand Equity goes behind the scenes with the strategists and creatives who produced a surprise advertising case-study**

Aarti Razdan

THE address 99, South Avenue in New Delhi has been the scene of celebrations recently, and a crowd of white-clad, jubilant Congressmen were toasting their success with ice-

ry with the win, and everyone in marketing and advertising circles are talking about the 'Aam aadmi...' campaign strategy.

There was no way the high-decibel India Shining juggernaut could be matched by the Congress, given its relatively paltry media budget of around Rs 20 crore. The

Brand Equity, Economic Times, 2004.

Given the decision to go regional, it was but natural to think vernacular. The entire campaign was conceived in Hindi and regional languages as opposed to the earlier trend of conceiving it first in English and then translating. One of the most successful campaign slogans ever used was 'Garibi Hatao' used by Indira Gandhi in 1971. While the party wanted something similar it was convinced that it had to shift from the 'Garibi Hatao' platform to a more "all inclusive" one. This shift of targeting the common man rather than the poor man resulted in the Aam aadmi campaign. It was the one theme that connected with a much wider audience and didn't alienate the middle class — something the 'Garibi Hatao' campaign is believed to have done. It is difficult to find who conceived the idea of *Aam aadmi ko kya mila*, as both the agency as well as the client are ready to stamp it as their original creation. Arvind Sharma, CEO and chairman, Leo Burnett, says that he played a role in coining the slogan — that too, en route to

another client meeting in Pune. However, Jayshree Sundar, executive director, Leo Burnett, insists on giving some of the credit to the new Mrs G saying. "It was Mrs Gandhi's idea to reflect the real India consistently throughout the campaign." Mrs Gandhi was keenly involved in the entire campaign along with Rahul and Priyanka Gandhi. "Rahul and Priyanka used to sit for hours on each of the posters and ads before signing them off," shares Ramesh.

Once it was decided that the Aam aadmi would do all the talking, the campaign went for the jugular. It raised issues that had touched the target audience's lives — be it the coffin scam, UTI scam, farmers' suicides, unemployment or the Gujarat riots. The campaign not only spoke the consumer's language but also brought out regional pangs with an authentic look and feel — different models were used for North and South India even if the subject matter of the ad was the same.

According to Leo Burnett, in the qualitative and quantitative researches that were done, there was a clear indication that the common man was feeling left out. Burnett conducted two waves of research, one, right at the beginning when they had won the account and two, at the fag end of the campaign, to check on recall and effectiveness. At both junctures, to their surprise, majority of the respondents reacted sharply "My life has not changed over the last five years", and "Congress should be given a chance."

In the end, like exit-pollsters, ad gurus also had to bite the dust. India Shining, the campaign which was praised to the skies in the marketing and advertising communities and expected to help the BJP coast to victory, did not connect with the common man. The Congress campaign which was barely noticed by ad-watchers and much less talked about, delivered the goods for the grand old party.

With Aam aadmi's blockbuster success, the party now has plans to extend the concept post-elections as well. But before going overboard on the strategy hype — both agency and client would do well to remember that when one wins, all actions leading up to it are called strategy and if one loses, the very same actions could be pilloried and consigned to the dustheap of history.

aarti.sardana@timesgroup.com

# Campaign Chemistry

From Page 1

Brand Equity, Economic Times, 2004.

NDA performance

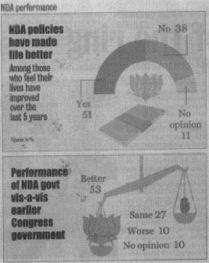

**NDA policies have made life better**

Among those who feel their lives have improved over the last 5 years

Figures in %

No 38

Yes 51

No opinion 11

**Performance of NDA govt vis-a-vis earlier Congress government**

Better 53

Same 27

Worse 10

No opinion 10

down to their own constituencies, but would be free to work upon the party cadres everywhere.

A key feature in working up the tempo of the cadres has been the role of the RSS. A top level meeting of RSS and BJP leaders at Prime Minister Vajpayee's residence in early March ensured the RSS's total support in the coming polls, in return for minor references to the RSS pet issues in the BJP's Vision Document. The minor frictions between the two in the past six years of NDA rule have all been forgotten. When Vishwa Hindu Parishad leaders like Giriraj Kishore and Pravin Togadia expressed their annoyance over the BJP's indifferent attitude to the Ram temple in its campaign, they were firmly silenced by the RSS. "Ever since Venkaiah Naidu took over as BJP president, he has tried to build a close rapport with the RSS at all levels," conceded RSS spokesman Ram Madhav. "This will certainly help the party now."

The same voices which are sceptical of Mahajan's computer-driven poll management style also insisted that the achievements the party initially touted in support of its 'feel-good' slogan had mainly benefited the urban middle classes; burgeoning foreign exchange reserves, new highways, more telephones. Prime Minister Vajpayee too lent weight to this view, which acquired a still sharper edge with the Congress riposte of Aam admi ko kya mila (What has the common man gained?). Accordingly, the BJP has made a midcourse correction in its propaganda content: the emphasis is firmly on achievements in rural India.

Even more than the Golden Quadrilateral highway project, it is the Rs 60,000-crore Gram Sadak Yojna of the NDA government which is being harped upon, along with rural credit cards, the Sampoorna Grameen Rozgar Yojna for rural employment, and the distribution of land to tribals. "Our government has done a great deal for the rural areas, but the media focus has been much greater on urban areas," said general secretary Mukhtar Abbas Naqvi. "In our campaign, we had to correct that."

BJP poll managers claimed to be always alert to the twin pitfalls of peaking too early, and an overkill of publicity. "We are well aware of the danger of becoming complacent, especially with all the opinion polls predicting an NDA victory," said vice-president Pyarelal Khandelwal. "It has been discussed at our meetings and we have warned our people accordingly." Again, to avoid overkill, for instance, a second shift of emphasis has been to reduce the number of advertisements the BJP had originally planned for the print media. The party is also looking much more closely now at the regional press, and smaller newspapers which reach semi-rural areas, than at the national press. Party leaders maintained that too many ads, coming in the wake of the earlier 'India Shining' campaign, were not being well received, and the budget was being diverted to the campaign itself.

The three super managers of the poll campaign are of course Naidu, Mahajan and Jaitley. Though Mahajan and Jaitley have been allotted specific states as well—Uttar Pradesh and Karnataka, respectively—surveys and opinion polls countrywide continue to remain their responsibility. General secretary Sanjay Joshi, a long-time RSS man, is chief troubleshooter for resolving organisational glitches, and Naqvi handles tour programmes. While Deputy Prime Minister Lal Krishna Advani's punishing Bharat Uday yatra continues, Vajpayee's public meetings—in such contrast to Sonia Gandhi's—have been deliberately rationed.

Keeping in mind his indifferent health, as well as to avoid overkill, Vajpayee will address no more than 40 meetings till the last phase of polls on May 10, the maximum number being in Uttar Pradesh, where the party is still unsure of its prospects. ◆

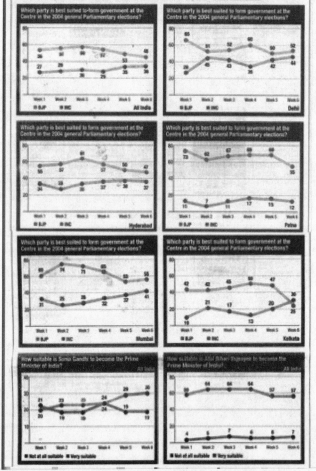

# TOI-TNS tracker: Cong finds new friends

Times News Network

New Delhi: While the preference for BJP to form the next government continued to drop in the last few weeks, the concomitant benefit appears to have gone to Congress, which many more people now believe is a fit party to rule from New Delhi.

According to a new survey conducted on behalf of *The Times of India* by TNS, while the party's stock in the national capital and Mumbai sta-

bilised slightly, more people seemed to have stepped off the fence in the two largest Indian cities to back Congress.

In Kolkata, Congress' popularity has in fact surged ahead of BJP's and in places such as Hyderabad and Patna, BJP's fortunes were on a downside.

Not surprisingly, Vajpayee's personal ratings seem to be closely tied to BJP's but the number of city folk

joining the ranks of Vajpayee-haters in the last few weeks has plateaued out, the survey showed.

Congress president Sonia Gandhi's favourability to be the next Indian PM, which started going up with the entry of Rahul Gandhi in the electoral ring and as Priyanka hit the campaign trail, was still inching upward, specially in New Delhi, Mumbai and, surprisingly, in Modi-controlled Ahmedabad.

While the preference for BJP to form the next government continued to drop in the last few weeks, the concomitant benefit appears to have gone to Congress, which many people now believe is a fit party to rule from New Delhi…Times of India survey. April 18th, 2004.

# Shoestring Cong campaign took shine off NDA's

**EXPRESS NEWS SERVICE**
NEW DELHI, MAY 15

THE NDA might have splurged on its "India Shining" campaign, but it was the Congress that worked doubly hard to wipe off the shine. In fact, according to AdEx India (Tam Media Research), in terms of advertising time, it was the Congress that came first followed by the Telugu Desam Party, and occupying third place was the BJP.

The Congress, with 60,000 seconds, topped the list, followed by the Telugu Desam Party with 40,000 seconds and the BJP with 29,000 seconds. However, in terms of money spent, the Congress, according to a report in the *Asian Wall Street Journal*, spent around $6.5 million to stage a comeback.

On the other hand, the NDA spent nearly $100 million. On the election campaign, the money spent by the BJP is close to Rs 100 crore.

"The low-budget message eventually won out," the report added.

The report said that Grey Global group's Indian division, which worked for the BJP, highlighted what it called a "feelgood factor" through a campaign called "India Shining", highlighting the government's role in the country's economic upswing.

The campaign — estimated to cost as much as $100 million — was so dominant on television that the phrase has worked its way into daily life, headlines and even other ads, the report said.

"In the other camp, Leo Burnett, via a wholly-owned local subsidiary called Orchard, worked for the Congress.

In its ads, the Congress pulled a different emotional lever, reaching out to poor rural voters who have not shared India's recent boom.

"What did the common man get?" asked ads featuring ordinary Indians.

Indian Express. May 15th, 2004.

Congress operations centre. The front door is perpetually locked to mislead the hangers-on and informers. "There is no dearth of those who come here and then pass on information to the other side [ read the BJP ]", says one of the acolytes. Those who come for business are allowed in through the backdoor. In one corner is a cut-out of

Day

**BRAINSTORMING: (From left) Jairam Ramesh, Salman Khurshid, Rajiv Shukla and Anand Sharma among others at the Congress election war room**

' SANJAY AHLAWAT

Sonia, head covered and hands folded in a 'namaste'. But it has been rejected because the colour of her sari is all wrong. It is a bright saffron.

On the wall in the main room are six basic posters that the Congress is printing from seven centres (decentralised for the first time) at Bangalore, Chandigarh, Delhi, Guwahati, Kolkata, Mumbai and Shimla. The party has also come out with a wall-size poster of Sonia in multimodes (with women, children, farmers and scientists) and the slogan in Hindi, 'Come let's make our nation great, let's build a new nation'. This is to form the backdrop of campaign meetings.

With the first phase of polling just

## Common man's agenda

What they need from a party in power

| | |
|---|---|
| Develop infrastructure | 18 |
| Reduce unemployment | 16 |
| Control price rise | 13 |
| Eradicate poverty | 12 |
| Ensure communal harmony | 5 |
| Resolve Ayodhya issue | 4 |
| Improve law & order | 4 |
| Bring development to my region | 4 |
| Others | 24 |

a fortnight away, the Congress is awaiting the results of a second survey it commissioned. It has launched the third phase of its ad campaign focusing on the manifesto and the 'Vision for the Future' outlined in it. This has the six basics for governance by the Congress: social cohesion and harmony; one crore jobs a year and at least one job per family; welfare of farmers and labourers; unleashing of the creative energies of professionals and entrepreneurs; political empowerment, educational, economic and legal equality for women; and equality of opportunity for Dalits, adivasis, OBCs and religious and linguistic minorities.

The strategists are most encouraged by the feedback they have on Sonia's Jan sampark (mass contact programme). Says Ramesh: "The party organisation should now convert the goodwill and enthusiasm generated through this programme into votes. Sonia Gandhi will move to the next

Coverage in the media of the posters created....
on the wall in the main room are six basic posters that the Congress is printing from seven centres...the party has also come out with a wall-size poster of Sonia in multi-modes (with women, children, farmers and scientists) and the slogan in Hindi. 'Come let's make our nation great, let's build a new nation.' This is to form the backdrop of campaign meetings...

# No bulky manifesto this time

By Our Special Correspondent

NEW DELHI, MARCH 22. Change is in the air ... or so the Congress hopes as it pulls all the stops out to come back to power at the Centre. Whether it will succeed will be known on May 13 or maybe even later in the eventuality of a hung Parliament. But, one thing is clear: The Congress is changing.

At least, its manifesto — released here today — was a far cry from the wordy text it brought out in 1999. In fact, the Congress president, Sonia Gandhi, herself acknowledged that this manifesto was different from previous ones during the question-answer session when mediapersons asked why the document did not have a component on foreign affairs. "We did not want to bring out a bulky manifesto," she quipped.

That it is a "time for change" was articulated by the Congress on the cover of the manifesto itself. Colourful with a picture of Ms. Gandhi working the crowds, the manifesto has been titled 'A Time for Change: Progress with Congress' and bears the party's new all-encompassing slogan "Congress ka Haath: Aam Aadmi Ke Saath."

Set in the party's colours with every turn carrying the slogan, photographs capturing vignettes of India in all its glorious diversity amid stark realities — as showcased by some of the party's own counter-advertisements to the 'India Shining' campaign — provide visual relief to the text.

As against the tightly-printed 80-page manifesto brought out in 1999, the manifesto this time round has been wrapped up in 32 pages. But, there is more to follow as three vision documents have been planned and each is likely to be released with considerable fanfare so that the party and its policies remain in public discourse.

---

…the Congress is changing. At least its manifesto – released yesterday - was a far cry from the wordy text it brought out in 1999…that it is a 'time for change' was articulated by the Congress on the cover of the manifesto itself...set in the party's colors with every turn carrying the slogan, photographs capturing vignettes of India in all its glorious diversity…provide relief to the text…

…the Congress is changing. At least its manifesto – released yesterday - was a far cry from the wordy text it brought out in 1999…that it is a 'time for change' was articulated by the Congress on the cover of the manifesto itself...set in the party's colours with every turn carrying the slogan, photographs capturing vignettes of India in all its glorious diversity…provide relief to the text…

— The Hindu

# Action-oriented manifesto, says

By Our Special Correspondent

NEW DELHI, MARCH 22. The Congress today described the coming Lok Sabha elections as a "clash of sharply competing values, of diametrically opposite ideologies" and against the Bharatiya Janata Party, which was "systematically undermining the very essence of Indian civilisation".

"The Congress' goal is to defeat the forces of obscurantism and bigotry who contributed nothing to the Freedom movement or the making of our Constitution and whose sole objective is to subvert our millennial heritage and composite nationhood," the party said in its 32-page manifesto.

Releasing the document, the party president, Sonia Gandhi, said it was packaged differently, action-oriented and transparent unlike the BJP whose real agenda was hidden behind the veneer of the National Democratic Alliance. As a measure of the party's commitment to implementation of the manifesto and accountability, she said every year on October 2, birth anniversary of Mahatma Gandhi, the Congress would bring out a progress report of its implementation.

Spread over five sections, the document provides an overview of 45 years of the party's achievements, the reasons for which the party should be voted back to power, the "failures" of the NDA/BJP, and the priorities plans and programmes of the Congress. In addition, over the next few days the party would

The Congress president, Sonia Gandhi, shows the party's manifesto at a press conference in New Delhi on Monday. — Photo: Shanker Chakravarty

publish "vision documents" on economic and political affairs, social empowerment, and national security and foreign affairs separately.

Listing the "monumental failures" of the BJP-led NDA Government, the document said the last five years were marked by massive unemployment, falling growth rates, acute distress

among farmers and farm labourers, compromised national security and social disharmony. Also, it accused the Government of subverting the school curricula, destroying probity, denigrating key institutions and undermining the independence of the foreign policy.

On the contentious Ayodhya issue, the manifesto said all par-

ties must wait for and abide by the verdict of the courts.

For minorities, the Congress pledged to extend reservation for the economically deprived persons belonging to communities that were at present not entitled to such reservation. It also promised to amend the Constitution to establish a commission for minority educational institu-

---

March 23rd, 2004....spread over five sections, the document provides an overview of the party's achievements, the reason for which the party should be voted back to power, the failures of the BJP/NDA govt., and the priorities plans, programmes of the Congress...

"Most of the credit being taken by the NDA government in the 'India Shining' campaign, from IT to economy to highways, are all results of the process set in motion by Congress governments since Rajiv Gandhi's time, and our manifesto will point this out," AICC secretary Jairam Ramesh, who is in the core team of the Congress election management team, confirmed.

The AICC is also preparing a media blitzkrieg, which has started with the "Aam Aadmi Ko Kya Mila (What the common man got during the NDA rule" campaign, targeting different groups of potential voters like the educated, unemployed youth, the marginalised and the weaker strata of the society.

The party high command, the sources said, is hoping to achieve through the campaign what it believes it has not been able to through the media campaign. "It is unfortunate but true that the media highlights only our attacks on the BJP, but not the positive things we are planning to do, and that is the gap we believe the ad campaign will be able to plug," the sources said.

However, with the BJP running ahead till now in media management vis-à-vis the elections, a section of the AICC leadership is understood to be not too happy with the delay in launching the publicity campaign.

According to sources, the Congress should have started not only the media campaign but also

> The AICC is also preparing a media blitzkrieg, which has started with the 'Aam Aadmi Ko Kya Mila' (what the common man got during the NDA rule) campaign, targeting different groups of potential voters like the educated, unemployed youth, the marginalized and the weaker strata of the society…

# 'Don't Forget 2004': Sonia Gandhi's Message To BJP

'Don't forget 2004,' she said, reminding the media of her party Congress taking power despite widespread predictions of a BJP victory.

Do you think PM Modi is invincible, reporters asked Sonia Gandhi, who was with her son and Congress president Rahul Gandhi outside the election office where she had come to file her documents.

'Not at all, not at all. Don't forget 2004,' Sonia Gandhi, the former Congress president, said. 'In 2004 (Atal Bihari) Vajpayee ji was also invincible but we won,' she added, walking away.

— Deccan Herald, 17 March, 2004.

# MRS G, KING-CONG SIZE

**Backed by 'youthful' photos and soundbytes proclaiming her as the embodiment of the late Rajiv Gandhi's soul, the Congress gives Sonia Gandhi a poll-perfect image makeover**

ARUN KUMAR DAS & NONA WALIA
Times News Network

Congress versus BJP. Sonia Gandhi versus Atal Behari Vajpayee. The war of the poses. It's official now. And like all great contests, it's come down to a photo-finish. Literally at that.

As new, styled snapshots of G get ready for display in the Congress office, the spotlight is on her 'Indianness'. Her look: Indian. Her mood: youthful. Her style: Sonia shining and Sonia smiling. Sonia's Indianness-Quotient will be the punchline for the party's ad campaign.

The minds behind the photo-shoots and her audio-video campaigns are Salman Khurshid, Jairam Ramesh, Ahmed Patel, Ambika Soni, Pranab Mukherjee, Manmohan Singh and Arjun Singh. Khurshid's backroom boys from LSE, Cambridge, Berkley and JNU have added the punch.

"We've prepared an ad campaign showing Mrs Gandhi as a youth leader compared to Atalji, who is on the wrong side of 75," says CWC member Khurshid, "It's all about being young this election, reaching out with energy."

As election fever grips the

**Congress' 'new' USP for Sonia**
- ■ Scores high with Indianness-Quotient
- ■ A 'youth' leader compared to Vajpayee
- ■ 'Karm jogini' as against 'goongi gudiya'

**CONGRESS CD SOUNDBYTES**

■ PARODY OF KAR CHALE HUM FIDA...

Kar chale hum fida jaan tan saathiyon...
Nazar aasinge mein Sonia yesh main,
yeh karegi hamara har swapn poora...
Rahul, Priyanka mein meri atmaan,
Inka andar mujhe dekhna saathiyon,
Yeh banayonge bharat ko dulhan saathiyon
*(Background image: Rajiv Gandhi)*

■ PARODY OF EK MACHCHAR NE AADMI KO...

Ek galat vote poora rashtra ko apahij bana
deta hai... ha, ha
*Voice: Nana Patekar clone*

the songs and SMSs the Congress has in store: 'BJP is stressing on stars 'cos its own stars are under stress'; 'Ye jo public hai sab janti hai, BJP kya hai, Tehelka kya hai, Judeo kya hai, tauba karo sab janti hai'. Says Khurshid, "Our strategy is two-pronged. In the first phase, there are nine posters, plus slogans, highlighting unemployment, the plight of farmers, and insecurity of women. Besides, there are SMSs, CDs and cassettes based on popular songs. In the second phase, we will showcase positive aspects of the Congress regime."

But that's not the end of the soundbytes. Congress poll CDs have images of Rajiv Gandhi making an appeal for Sonia, Priyanka and Rahul set to the tune of *Kar chale hum fida* and a parody spoofed from Nana Patekar's famous lines in the film *Yashwant: Ek machchar ne aadmi ko...*

"Compared to the last elections, there's a big change in how we're going to project Mrs Gandhi's image. Last time, it was just rallies. This time, she'll make a mass contact," says AICC secretary campaign Jairam Ramesh, "She's already more accessible to the media." And Rahul, Priyanka? They aren't really visible in the Congress posters or ad campaigns being prepared. "It's too early to come to conclusions," says a Congress worker, "This is only the beginning." It must certainly is. Because, even if the war of the poses gets nobody's vote, the Games have begun.

*Photo: Nana Patekar clone*

---

As new styled snapshots of Mrs. G get ready for display in the Congress office, the spotlight is on her 'Indianness'. Her look: Indian. Herstyle: Sonia shining and Sonia smiling…we've prepared an ad campaign showing Mrs. Gandhi as a youth leader compared to Atalji, who is on the wrong side of 75….

# Cong's feel-bad factor

**FRANKLY YOURS**
DINA NATH MISHRA

Of late the Congress has realised that denial of 'feel-good' would not work. Its strategists have started conceding 'half feel-good' and posing a question: 'Aam Aadmi ko Kya Mila'…

— The Pioneer, 14th March.

BJP's voice mails having Prime Minister A B Vajpayee's message.

"Ours is a low cost campaign, with no frills," says Ramesh. He adds that the party's national campaign will be divided into a 30:70 ratio of attacking the BJP and highlighting the Congress party's policies and work. At the state level, the party will concentrate on attacking the government wherever it is not in power and highlighting the achievements where it is in power. "For example, in Andhra Pradesh, we will attack the Chandrababu Naidu regime, while in Karnataka we will project all the good work the Krishna government has done," says Ramesh.

The party has also come up with some innovative slogans to be incorporated in a set of nine posters. The slogans vary from the emotive to the political. One of the posters, with six carefully selected photographs of Sonia Gandhi and a shot of Rajiv Gandhi, says, "Aaiye, banaye desh mahaan, karein rashtra ka nav nirman" (Come, let's join hands to develop a great country, to build a new nation), while another directly attacks the BJP, "Akhir weh log ek mahila se darte kyon hain?" (After all, why are they afraid of one woman?)

Some of the other slogans include promises to unemployed youths, women and farmers, keeping in mind the Congress president's thrust on campaign issues relating to farmers and the unemployed. The party has also appointed a public relations firm called Perfect Relations to take care of the media's needs vis-à-vis information on election-related developments. Hardened journalists say its inexperience in handling a political account is clearly showing as it is sending out only some basic information and soliciting scribes for interviews with party spokespersons with whom they interact on a daily basis throughout the year on a regular basis anyway.

## Reports in Deccan herald 14th March.

crescendo in the next few weeks. The AICC has also…the Congress strategy makers are confident that their party will make its point through a no-frills publicity campaign that has already begun in a low key manner through the 'Aam Admi Ko Kya Mila' series on newspaper adverts, which will reach its crescendo in the next few weeks. The AICC has also got series of attractive posters designed by the agency…

…the Congress strategy makers are confident that their party will make its point through a no-frills publicity campaign that has already begun in a low key manner through the 'Aam Admi Ko Kya Mila' series on newspaper advts, which will reach its got series of attractive posters designed by the agency…

India's top six political slogans and their impact
Congress ka Haath, AamAadmikeSaath

The Congress campaign that trumped BJP's India Shining in 2004. Once again India's Grand Old Party targeted India's common man to come back to power. It was a variation of an earlier Congress slogan that had 'garibkesaath'. The 'aamaadmi' was to include India's growing middle class.
— Economic Times, October 6, 2013.

# It's a no-frills campaign

Deccan Herald, Sunday, March 14, 2004

**The Congress party's publicity strategists are trying hard to remove the sheen off the India Shining campaign. But it is lagging behind.**

Utpal Borpujari in New Delhi

Remember the song, or is it a recitation, by Nana Patekar in a Hindi film some years ago which went like this: "Ek macchar aadmi ko..."? Now, the same song comes in handy for the Congress, for whom a person whose voice sounds uncannily like Patekar's, sings : "Ek galat vote rashtra ko apahij bana deta hai" (one wrong vote leaves the country disabled. The song is in a set of compact discs that the party's media and publicity strategists will use to spread the Congress message to every nook and corner of the country, besides the usual publicity material like posters, banners and the like.

The Sonia Gandhi-led party, however, is clearly lagging behind its main rival, the BJP, as far as taking the party message to the voters goes. While the BJP has cashed in on the advantage of being the party in power with the 'India Shining' campaign ostensibly to publicise what the Vajpayee government's achievements were, Deputy Prime Minister L K Advani has taken it to the next stage by launching the 'Bharat Uday Yatra' to take the same message directly to the people. Though somewhat worried over what it alleges is a massive misuse of public money in the 'India Shining' campaign, the Congress strategy makers are confident that their party will be able to make its point through a no-frills publicity campaign that has already begun in a low key manner through the 'Aam aadmi ko kya mila' series of newspaper advertisements which will reach its crescendo in the next few weeks.

While the AICC publicity department has got a series of attractive posters designed by the Orchard advertising agency that has bagged the party account, the party has also decided to make use of the public's craze for cinema by using video vans and cine-theatres to show a series of party related films. At the same time, a series of audio CDs, like the one in which Patekar mimics, will blare loudly and clearly, attacking the BJP and its allies and espousing the Congress cause.

Aware that the party cannot match the ruling side's spending power – AICC leaders involved in

— Deccan Herald, March 14th, 2004.

☰          **WSJ**          🔍

# Global Ad Agencies Brought 'Branding' to India's Election

*By Geoffrey A. Fowler* Staff Reporter of *THE WALL STREET JOURNAL*
Updated May 14, 2004 12:01 am ET

🔖 SAVE    ➥ SHARE    A͓A TEXT

Two of Madison Avenue's biggest advertising agencies have brought India's 670 million voters a new, albeit influential, nuisance: political ads.

For the first time in the country's history, campaign ads leading up to parliamentary elections outnumbered all other ad categories on Indian television, save for a few times when ads for "All Out" bug repellent reigned.

The ad shops were more than prolific. In teaming up with India's two dominant parties at a time of rapid change, they also helped articulate opposing

←    →    ⊕    78    •••

Jairam Ramesh and Rupam Borah at 99 South Avenue. The war room. Plastered with maps and creative output.

The author at 99 South Avenue—against the backdrop of the manifesto and Impact features.

Ali Imran at 99 South Avenue with a cross section of the print ads and posters and campaign material as the backdrop.

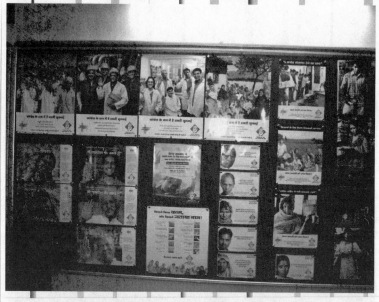

The print ads of the 2004 Congress campaign up on the war room softboards.

Ali Imran, Shamim Akhtar, Rupam Borah.

Mrs. Sonia Gandhi's poster campaign.

Salman Khurshid and Jairam Ramesh cutting the hand cake at our office.

Jairam Ramesh, Anita Nayyar, Rupam Borah at a small tea at our office where the client finally came over once the campaign ended.

Creative posters created by Rupam — fun depictions - This one for Jairam Ramesh who always told us, "I am not into micromanagement - just do it - but no mistakes permitted".

A similar poster created for Salman Khurshid who always signed off the creative from the clients end.

The Congress Leaders at our office during cake cutting after the victory.

## cover story BUILDING AN INDIAN CENTURY

responsibility to change the nature and course of our politics. Cynicism about politics and politicians is dangerous and can subvert the very foundations of our democracy. Elections provide the oxygen to keep our democracy going. But politics of our country has to rediscover for itself a higher sense of moral purpose that goes beyond mere numbers. Politics must be grounded in core values that provide direction and inspiration and that bind the country together. Politics must be more than the pursuit of power.

It must be, as it was once, all about service and sacrifice. It must attract and retain the best and the brightest. It must not only offer hope that gets renewed from time to time but it must also fulfil the expectations and aspirations of people—of the *Aaam Aadmi* (common man), I might add.

A continuing Indian century must be one in which every Indian, particularly those from the deprived and disadvantaged sections of society, can both participate and partake. The continuing Indian century will undoubtedly come from the exuberance, energy and enterprise of its youth, of its women, of its entrepreneurs, of its civil society. Yet, it will also demand a whole new vision for the state, a whole new definition of its role and responsibilities. This vision must give the state a new strength and im-

part to
century
not rest
the syn
tions th

*Sonia Ga*

Cover Story: Building an Indian Century.

The leadership team at Leo Burnett Delhi 2004.Jayshree, Ali, Rupam.

# ACKNOWLEDGEMENTS

At the tail end of a family zoom call in July 2020, I floated the idea of a book I was planning to write. My niece Moina and her husband Amol were the ones who hadn't logged out as yet. I asked if I could read out the first chapter I had written. As I was halfway, I could see Amol totally engaged and Moina distracted. When I finished, Moina said, 'But I thought you should write about the Congress campaign. After all, how many people can tell that story?'

It set me thinking. I changed track as you can see and, therefore, I credit Moina with the idea of this book. Thanks, my Moinoo.

And while the details are fresh in my head, and since I teach it like a case study as a part of MBA curriculum, I was sure of the chronology of events. My students enjoying it and learning so much from it validated my point that the story was very relevant today and would be in times to come. So, a big shout out to all of you.

I formed a WhatsApp group and got my 2004 team together. They were wondering what was going on! Excited to see and meet in a 'work situation' after so many years. Once I revealed the idea of the book, there was unanimous excitement.

People started talking at the same time animatedly. So many stories, so many experiences. They were generous with their time and support. Rupam, Anita, Ali, Kosty, Pooja, Kabir and Prantik. 'It's our book' Prantik said and everyone embodied that spirit.

My entire office at LB Delhi—You guys were a star team. What magic we created together!

My niece Debjani, who was the first one to read the full manuscript and call me from Dubai excitedly. She said it was an easy read and she loved the portrayal of the agency life. I asked her to read it first as I wanted a young person's feedback who has low interest in politics. Passing the test with her as she is an avid reader made me feel good. Thanks, Toofy!

My sister Mita who was checking on my progress with the book one day and offered to read the draft and give me her feedback. She stayed a couple of weeks in my house in the winter of 2004 and saw this unfold in front of her eyes. Sitting past midnight in the freezing cold in the car, waiting for me to emerge from various meetings so that she could get some time with me. She messaged after reading the first few pages and said, 'It's going great so far…' She also helped with some editing and suggestions.

Pooja told me at the outset she would design the cover, and one month after we had started our discussions she and I met on a virtual call where she showed me four fantastic cover designs. The one you see is the first option she presented. I loved it. Kosty joined us on these calls and we discussed a lot of issues, structure, material. A few weeks later Ali also joined in. Kosty and Ali read through the entire book and edited and corrected it. Like I said, with a team like this I did'nt need to look outside for help. Ali also shared all the material he had and that was really useful. Thanks, guys.

Thanks also to my publisher Vitasta for bringing this case study to everyone. In particular to Managing Director Renu Kaul Verma who was such a good partner to collaborate with. Who understood that this was a unique story that would be important to tell. Very open to discussion and totally encouraging all the way. Also Manjula Lal, seasoned journalist, who edited the manuscript. Thanks for some very valuable suggestions and insights which helped to tighten the manuscript.

To my brother Probir who said, 'Don't worry about promoting your book. I will.' Blind faith! What more could a sister ask for?

My daughter Tarini. One morning I woke up to a message from her saying, 'Mom I've read 30 pages—it's a thriller'. She has pushed me and corrected copy and patiently heard my updates. Thanks darling. You inspire me every day.

My husband Sundar. Who read drafts. Typed a bit on days I was tired. Listened to the daily writing as I read it out to him and generally gave me my space to work quietly. Sometimes propping me up with a hot cup of tea. You know what you mean to me.

My parents. Thank god I was born to you. Both of you were brilliant. Your values and approach to life have been truly exemplary and my guiding light.

My in-laws. Thank you for all the encouragement you gave me as a working woman and showering me with praise for even the smallest achievements. You both had a very modern outlook.

And, finally, Lintas and Leo Burnett, two amazing agencies—thank you for teaching me everything I know in my professional field.